Brighton Publications, Inc.

75
<u>ICEBREAKERS</u>
FOR GREAT GATHERINGS

EVERYTHING
YOU NEED TO
BRING PEOPLE
TOGETHER

Nan Booth

Brighton Publications

Brighton Publications

Copyright © 1999 by Nan Booth

Brighton Publications, Inc.
P.O. Box 120706
St. Paul, MN 55112-0706
612-636-2220
800/536-2665
www.partybooks.com

First Edition: 2000

Library of Congress Cataloging-in-Publication Data
Booth, Nan
    75 Icebreakers for Great Gatherings : everything you need to bring people together / Nan Booth. — 1st ed.
        p. cm.
    Includes index.
    ISBN 0-918420-34-2 (paperback)
    1. Group relations training. 2. Group facilitation. 3. Group games. I. Title: Seventy-five icebreakers for great gatherings. II. Title: 75 ice breakers for great gatherings. III. Title: Seventy-five ice breakers for great gatherings.

HM1086.B66 2000
302'.14—dc21   99-059326

Printed in the United States of America

TABLE OF CONTENTS

CHAPTER FOUR: ICEBREAKERS FOR FUN / 106

Sometimes, all you need is fun. Take a few minutes just to play. Play indoors, play outdoors. Play word games, play physical games. Play silly games. Get loose.

PLAYING WITH WORDS / 100

ALL-PURPOSE, ALL OCCASION / 108

DEPARTMENT OF SILLY GAMES / 117

Introduction ____

ABOUT ICEBREAKERS

As a general term, "icebreaker" means different things to different people. Enter it into your computer's search engine, for example, and you get information likely to be useful to arctic explorers and winter fishing enthusiasts, among other things. A widely accepted meaning, and the one this book is about, has to do with icebreakers as tools which allow group leaders, in either professional or social capacities, to encourage and enhance interaction among participants.

As such, icebreakers can serve as introductions to new people and to new ideas, as stimulants to creative thinking, as transitions from one topic to another, and as changes of pace during the course of an event. They are effective at the beginning, at various times throughout, and at the end as a way to provide closure. Energizers and warm-ups are related terms with similar meanings.

Icebreakers can help members of a group get to know each other quickly, and get to know a leader or important guests more easily. They can point towards a learning topic of the day, or towards a shared task, increasing interest and participation. They can allow for exploration of new ideas, of first impressions, of backgrounds and ideas, and of goals and interests. Further, icebreakers are fun, and are often most successfully used with no other purpose than that.

Useful and versatile as they are, however, the decision to use an ice-breaker, as well as the decision as to which icebreaker to use in which situation, should never be made lightly. They have unintended as well as intended results, and both will vary widely depending on the nature of the group and the event. Icebreakers help create the ambiance and set the tone. Know your group, know the purpose of the event, and choose an icebreaker that is congruent with both.

This is no simple matter, however. Choosing a serious-minded ice-breaker for a serious-minded event might accomplish the on-task purpose, but also send the unintended message that no fun, and per-haps no spontaneity or creativity, will be tolerated. Choosing a light-hearted icebreaker for the same event might be exactly the right touch of humor and whimsy, or it might strike participants as a frivolous waste of time, and backfire completely. Think it through in the light of all the information you have, and choose wisely.

Consider safety, psychological as well as physical. Icebreakers are intended to increase participants' comfort level, but may well have the exact opposite effect for some people in some circumstances. State clearly that no one will be required to participate. Explain the reason for this icebreaker at this time. Explain what the icebreaker entails. Ask for questions about it. If it involves intense or complex physical activity, or personal revelations and interactions that might be difficult for some to engage in, allow for different levels of participation. Providing options often increases both participation and enjoyment.

In this book, Chapter One contains icebreakers for various pur-poses, and all of them can be completed in under ten minutes. Icebreakers commonly serve as introductions, and Chapter Two con-tains a good selection. The icebreakers in Chapter Three are meant for use on special occasions, from corporate retreats to family reunions. Chapter Four contains nothing but fun.

All of the icebreakers are preceded by a brief explanation of what size group they are intended for, approximately how long they will take, and what prior planning and materials they require. These are all meant as suggestions. Most of the icebreakers can be adapted somehow for groups of most sizes. Many require little or nothing in the way of planning or materials. Read them through, engage your own creative ingenuity, consult your experience and preferences, and decide which are right for your situation.

By their nature, icebreakers are short. Except in Chapter One, each icebreaker is described as having a short, medium, or long time frame. These terms are relative. Short might be five to ten minutes, medium ten to fifteen minutes, and long about twenty minutes. Most, however, can be adapted to your group's needs and preferences, to fill time as needed or to provide a quick transition or refocus.

Once you read the icebreakers presented here, and consider their possibilities for your group and your event, you make them your own. They are not recipes or formulas, any deviation from which will result in disaster. Rather, they are living, breathing, growing, changing, adaptable, organic, and nearly endlessly variable. Twist them, turn them, inside out, upside down, shape them, mold them, make them fit, make them suitable only for your group in its particular situation at this particular time; add a goal where there is none, get rid of the goal and make it only for fun, change the theme, create a new theme, do whatever you want. And have fun.

Chapter
1

ICEBREAKERS IN TEN MINUTES OR LESS

• •

Most of us are familiar with the feeling of having too much to do and too little time to do it in. Whether we are planning our own day or a get-together with others, no matter how much time is available, it isn't enough. The agenda may be packed or sparse, but we rarely seem to get through it all. One of Murphy's Laws may apply here — "work expands to fill the time available" — or maybe something in human nature works against effective time management. Then again, maybe it's a matter of excitement and exuberance: we have so much to do, to learn, to pass on, to share, to accomplish, to enjoy.

Conversely, time tends to drag, even in those work, learning, or social situations in which we have a high level of interest and a high stake. After a while, we lose our focus, we get hungry or sleepy, we need to move around, we want to get to the next part, we forget the purpose or the goal, or we no longer care. It might be time to go home, but more likely it's time to break things up a bit in order to regain concentration and enthusiasm.

Icebreakers — short, snappy icebreakers, carefully chosen for the event and the audience, as well as for the tone they set — offer at least a partial solution to both problems. Get acquainted and get comfortable right away. Waste no time on lengthy lead-ins, just cut to the chase. Shake off the mid-session doldrums with a quick mental or physical refocusing technique. Icebreakers in ten minutes or less save you time, and keep your event on track and interesting.

Ten-Minute Starters

These offer quick ways to introduce participants to each other and to the subject matter. They help overcome the initial inertia inherent in group situations, and help put participants at ease. Most work with a group of any size, and require little in the way of props, materials, or planning.

Hats

Checklist

Group Size: any size; divide a very large group into smaller groups of 15 or fewer

Advance Preparation: none

Materials: large sheets of blank newsprint, markers if desired, enough for each participant

Give all participants a square of newsprint, and instruct them to make a hat from it. No further instructions are necessary, as each person may fold and pleat and crimp and crumple to the dictates of his or her creativity. If you provide markers, participants may choose to decorate their hats in some way, or write their names in a visible place on them.

Allow just a few minutes for the hat-making, then ask participants to model their hats while they introduce themselves to each other, exchanging names and, if they like, hat-making techniques.

Take the free-for-all approach to introductions, in which you allow five minutes for that purpose, asking participants to mingle. Or, take a more formal approach, and allow a brief turn for each person.

Make the activity slightly more elaborate by supplying such materials as tape or staplers, glue, glitter, colored markers, or bits of ribbon. Instead of newsprint, you could use felt or another fabric, paper grocery bags, or sheets of colored construction paper. In any case, don't get bogged down in the hat making, so you can move quickly to introductions.

Name Tags

Checklist

Group size: any size

Advance preparation: make a name tag for each participant

Materials: prepared name tags

Have the name tags in a handy place near the entrance, but keep them out of sight in a box or drawer. As each participant enters, ask his or her name, and check it off on the guest-list, if you have one. Then hand the participant someone else's name tag.

Some people may simply attach the name tag and move on, unaware that they are no longer quite themselves. Most people, however, will point out that you seem to have made a mistake. Explain that there is no mistake; no one has the correct name tag, and searching it out will help people meet each other more quickly.

Allow the activity to go on for a few minutes into the scheduled time, then ask those who have not found their own name tag to identify themselves. Make any exchanges — and introductions — necessary.

Wizard

Checklist

Group size: any size

Advance preparation: designate one or more "wizards;" post signs as described below

Materials: marbles, polished stones, buttons, pennies, or some other small token to represent "crystal balls."

Ahead of time, designate a wizard, or several wizards if the group is very large. Each wizard will carry a hidden supply of "crystal balls," and will secretly slip one into the palm of each person who approaches to shake hands. The wizards must do their best not to reveal themselves as they carry out their task.

Post a sign at the entrance, and several signs throughout the space, that encourage participants to mingle and shake lots of hands: "Shake the wizard's hand — get your crystal ball," "Have you met the wizard yet?" "Introduce yourself to the wizard!"

As each person enters, explain that a secret wizard is present; those who find and shake hands with the wizard will be rewarded with the gift of a crystal ball. They must, however, be sworn to secrecy, because wizards are very touchy about having their identities revealed indiscriminately.

Stop the activity after five or ten minutes. By that time the wizard's identity may well be common knowledge. Most people should be in possession of a crystal ball, and they have had a chance to meet and shake hands with lots of their fellow participants.

Memory

Ask all participants to find a partner whom they have not met, or don't know well. They should introduce themselves, and talk briefly.

After a minute or two, stop conversation, and ask the partners to stand back to back. Hand each person a memory card and a pencil.

The memory cards, prepared in advance on recipe cards or slips of paper, contain four or five questions related to appearance, such as the following:

Wearing glasses?

Wearing one or more earrings?

Wearing the color blue?

Hair parted left, right, center, or not at all?

Clothing style casual, business-like, or dressy?

Without turning around to look at each other, the partners should do their best to recall each other's appearance, and write accurate answers to the questions. When both have done so, they may turn around and check with each other to see how many items they remembered correctly.

Awards

Ahead of time, make one "award" for each participant: use yellow construction paper, and cut a shape like a medal or badge of honor; or, use blue construction paper, and cut a shape like a blue ribbon. The awards should be approximately 4 x 6 inches in size. Give each participant an award, a pen or marker, and a pin.

Offer examples of everyday things people do that are deserving of recognition: bring children to karate class faithfully twice a week, coach t-ball, stick to an exercise program, refrain from rolling eyes at partner's oft-repeated observations on the world, make home-made cakes from scratch for family birthdays, achieve perfect attendance at work. If you like, make your examples congruent with the nature or purpose of your get-together.

Allow two to three minutes for participants to write their names on their awards, followed by one or two things they do for which they feel they deserve a medal.

Then, one person starts by reading the name and accomplishments of the person to his or her left, and pinning that person's award on him or her. Continue until everyone has been introduced.

Real Questions

Explain that you want to speed up the introduction process by getting rid of the cliché part. The usual "How ya doin'," followed by a quick handshake and a blank look, doesn't do much to build relationships.

Instead, ask participants to prepare for a few minutes of mingling and introductions by writing down three "real" questions — things they actually would want to know about someone they are just meeting.

Give examples, which could range from the ordinary and mundane to the edges of psychotherapy:

Are you a dog person or a cat person? Do you play tennis? Do the names Mark McGuire and Sammy Sosa have any significance to you? Where did you grow up? What's your favorite restaurant? What was your childhood like? How's your love life? How do you spend your free time? What have you done that you're most proud of? That you're ashamed of? Can you laugh at yourself? Do you have a really good recipe for cheesecake, and if so, will you share it?

Allow about five minutes for participants to circulate and engage in brief conversations based on the questions they wrote down. The goal here is not to meet as many people as possible, but to really meet a few.

Handshake

Checklist

Group size: any size; a large group should be divided into smaller groups of up to ten

Advance preparation: none

Materials: none

A secret handshake is a fun way to establish group identity and membership. Tell participants that they will have an opportunity to develop their very own secret handshake, known only to them, that they can use whenever they want throughout the day or the event.

With a co-leader or volunteer, demonstrate some moves that might make up a secret handshake: various hand placements, touching elbows, twining fingers, grasping wrists, and so on. You could get creative and add hip bumps, belly thumps, or exclamations — Yeah! All right! Woo-oo!

Divide a large group into "teams" of no more than ten, so that each person will have a chance to contribute an idea. The handshake routine can be as elaborate or as simple as participants desire, but they have only a couple of minutes to develop it and practice it.

Once everyone on the team seems familiar with the secret handshake, participants use it as they introduce themselves to each other. If there are several teams, each team could also demonstrate its handshake for the larger group, with brief introductions.

Encourage participants to use their handshake whenever they can, such as after breaks or as a congratulatory gesture after accomplishing something.

Playing

Explain that a situation might arise during the event which could require an emergency play period, and that participants need to prepare. Give examples of various forms of play. Point out the differences between physical and childish forms of play, like skipping rope and hopscotch, and mental and serious forms of play, like bridge or chess.

Mention imaginative games like dress-up or cops and robbers. Mention playing at the beach, playing sports, making a hideout, dancing, hanging out with friends, arts and crafts, board games, telling jokes, eating, bicycling, going to the mall, and on and on and on.

Encourage participants to think about play, as children and now. Do they play for the competition, for the exercise, for the companionship, for the fun?

After a couple of minutes of discussion, ask each group to come up with an emergency play plan for the day. Since you have no materials or equipment, they will probably have to rely on long buried childhood instincts. One group might think of a quick round of freeze tag, and another a game of hide-and-seek. Others might come up with an imaginary expedition to some exotic place, skipping races, or a conga line.

Before beginning your planned agenda, spend a couple of minutes playing one group's selection, and save the others for later in the session.

Ten-Minute Energizers

When things bog down, as they inevitably do, you need a way to refocus and refresh, a way to shake off the doldrums and get back on track. Quick energizers help do that, without taking time away from a busy agenda.

Dictators

Checklist

Group size: any size, better with at least 15 people, divided into groups of four or five

Advance preparation: none

Materials: none

To divide into groups of four or five, have participants number off, group them according to where people are sitting, ask people to group themselves, randomly assign them to groups, or use any method of your choice that works quickly.

Once groups are formed, each must choose a leader. The leader could be the person wearing the brightest clothing, the person carrying the most pocket change, the tallest person, or the person whose birthday is closest to the current date; designate some such method, and have all of the small groups use it.

Each leader is a dictator, with absolute power over his or her citizens. Certain limitations apply to how the power may be used, however. While the citizens must carry out the dictator's orders unquestioningly, the dictator may only issue orders designed to promote the general good.

A dictator may, for example, send all of his or her citizens to neighboring groups with strict instructions to compliment everyone there, or to bestow pats on the back or some other form of encouragement, or to tell a joke, or offer neck massages, or lead a song.

Encourage dictators to think creatively about ways to promote peace, happiness, and good will in the gathering as a whole. Stop the activity and reconvene after about 5 minutes.

Fleas

Checklist

Group size: any size; break a large group into smaller groups of no more than 10

Advance preparation: none

Materials: none

Ask participants to stand in a circle facing each other. Explain that each person present has some sort of malady that seems to be affecting the group. Then say, "For instance, I have fleas," and start scratching behind one ear like a dog. Everyone in the circle must do the same.

Maybe the next person in the circle has the hops; everyone must then hop up and down on one foot while scratching behind one ear like a dog. If the next person has a hand tremor, then everyone must shake one hand while hopping up and down on one foot and scratching behind one ear like a dog.

If the next person is temporarily paralyzed, then everyone may mercifully stop moving altogether, until the next person announces an uncontrollable urge to do the twist, and the person after that has an eye twitch.

Continue until everyone in the circle has had a chance to display a "malady," and the group has experienced as many of them simultaneously as possible.

Compliments

Checklist

Group size: any size

Advance preparation: none

Materials: none

Randomly pair up participants. It doesn't matter if they know each other or not. Allow a couple of minutes for casual conversation, then ask for quiet. Ask each person to think of something complimentary to say to his or her partner.

Leave the nature of the compliment wide open, or make it specific, with regard to behavior, personality, role in the group or organization, or contributions to the group or organization.

Allow partners one minute each to compliment each other, then reconvene the group and go about your business.

Story

> ## Checklist
>
> Group size: up to about 20
>
> Advance preparation: none
>
> Materials: none

Explain that as a way to stimulate collective creativity, the group will make up a story. Each person, in turn, will tell a small portion of it. The process is similar to brainstorming, in that spontaneity and quantity of ideas are valued more highly than over-all quality, and no judgments may be made of anyone's contribution

A good story has a beginning, a middle, and an end. As your story makes its way from person to person around the room, those at the beginning set the scene, introduce characters, and establish a conflict or problem; those in the middle develop the plot; and those near the end figure out a way to wind it down.

One person starts at the beginning: "Once upon a time, a group of accountants became hopelessly lost in the woods. Their leader, a tough CPA named Vera, thought she knew these woods very well, because just two weeks ago she had lost at least half a dozen golf balls in them."

The next person continues, "Unfortunately, the group had wandered far from the deep rough on the left side of the fairway, and they had no idea where they were. Rob, a young accounting student, was tired, in great need of a beer, and unimpressed with Vera's leadership. He approached her and said...."

The third person picks it up there. Since the success of this activity depends on moving it along quickly, no one person should say more than two or three sentences, and no one should have too much time to think. One person must start talking as soon as the preceding person stops. Offering a word or two to help someone who is stuck is permissible. Breaking in on someone who goes on too long is also is permissible.

Use this as pure entertainment, or establish a theme that connects it to the purpose and nature of your get together.

T-shirts

Checklist

Group size: any size

Advance preparation: none

Materials: plain sheets of letter-sized paper, markers, straight pins

Set out the materials in an accessible location, and ask all participants to help themselves to one sheet of paper, their choice of markers, and two straight pins.

Ask participants to think about all the different messages they have seen on T-shirts, from simple advertising, to pithy comments about life, to comical self-disclosures, to risqué or even offensive remarks. They now have a chance to create their own T-shirt messages.

The messages can be in the form of instructions or advice to others, disclosures about oneself, comments on the days' proceedings, or observations about life in general. They can include simple drawings or visual images. Subject matter could be limited to topics related to the group and its purpose, or it could be left wide open.

GIVE A FEW EXAMPLES:

Crabby When Hungry — When's Lunch?

Creativity Gym — Flex Your Muscle

Life is Short — Play for Keeps

The Mom Formerly Known as Princess

After participants have created their T-shirts on the paper provided, they can pin them to their fronts as conversation starters for the rest of the event.

Catch

Checklist

Group size: any size; divide large groups into smaller groups of 12 to 15

Advance preparation: none

Materials: one large, soft, catchable ball; a minute and second timer, or a tape player with music

Designate someone to attend to the timer or the tape player; that person cannot otherwise participate in the activity. When asked, he or she will set the timer or play the music for short, random time periods, from about twenty seconds up to maybe ninety seconds.

Ask participants to stand in a circle, and take a few seconds to stretch and shake their arms and legs.

Start by throwing the ball back and forth with one other person. Expand the pattern of throwing and catching one person at a time, until the entire circle is involved. Try to make sure that no one receives the ball more often than anyone else.

Once group members are easily and casually throwing the ball around, set the timer or start the music; mention the childhood game of "hot potato," and say that whoever has possession of the ball when the timer goes off or the music stops is out.

The pace of play is likely to accelerate dramatically. Continue playing until at least three or four people are out, then go on to the next agenda item.

Changes

Checklist

Group size: any size, better with at least 12 people

Advance preparation: none

Materials: none

Gather in small groups of 4 or 5. Ask group members to take a few minutes to simply observe each other, noting what the others are wearing, their jewelry, shoes, hair styles, and so on.

Then, in a sort of fruit-basket-upset, ask all the small groups to disperse, and the members to mill around for a few minutes among the group as a whole. If your gathering is small, making it difficult for people to disappear into the crowd, ask them to face away from each other, so none of them can see the others.

Participants should then surreptitiously make several small changes to their appearance: remove a hair clasp or earrings, change a bracelet or watch to the other wrist, button up a sweater or jacket, untie a scarf or tie, roll sleeves up, tuck in a shirt tail, turn a cap from frontwards to backwards, and so on.

After a couple of minutes, ask participants to return to their small groups, or to turn around and face each other. As a group, see how many changes members can find in each other's appearance.

Laughing

Checklist

Group size: up to about 25 or 30

Advance preparation: none

Materials: none

This is a quick, spontaneous, and effective energizer. Unfortunately, its stated goal — to complete the entire activity with no laughter — is nearly impossible to achieve.

Start in whatever seating arrangement the group happens to be in — a circle, at tables, in rows, at random.

One person says "ha." The next person says "ha ha." The third person says "ha ha ha." Continue in order until everyone has said the required number of "ha's," moving as quickly as possible through the room.

Keeping track of how many times to say "ha" can become as difficult as refraining from laughter. To make it easier, when someone laughs, give that person a second chance; let him or her start with one "ha," and proceed as above.

If your group is sufficiently loose and informal, try this activity while lying on your backs on the floor. You won't be able to get past two or three "ha's" without someone laughing.

Ten-Minute Task Enhancers

Tasks, such as forming small groups, building teams, communicating effectively, or solving problems, sometimes slow things down, and sometimes derail a gathering altogether. Lively or thought-provoking icebreakers help groups carry out these and other tasks efficiently and pleasantly.

Sundaes

Checklist

Group size: any size

Advance preparation: make ingredient cards, as described below

Materials: ingredient cards

Use this icebreaker to divide your gathering into small groups. Prepare ahead of time by making as many ingredient cards as you will need. If you have a group of forty, and you want ten groups of four, make ten ice cream cards, ten chocolate syrup cards, ten butterscotch sauce cards, and ten nuts cards. Use pictures of the ingredients, or words.

Hand out the cards randomly. Ask participants to join with three other people so that together they have the necessary ingredients to make a chocolate-butterscotch sundae with nuts on top. If you need smaller or larger groupings, add or subtract sundae ingredients accordingly.

For a healthier gathering, make fruit salad instead of sundaes. Your salad could consist of watermelon, cantaloupe, and pineapple, if you need groups of three. If you need groups of ten, try peaches, blueberries, red grapes, kiwi fruit, raspberries, pears, honeydew, green grapes, strawberries, and plums.

Dog Face

Checklist

Group size: any size

Advance preparation: dog faces, as described below

Materials: cut out dog facial parts

Find a several pictures of dog faces; magazines, newspaper ads, calendars, or greeting cards are all good sources. You need one dog face for each small group you want to form. You could draw your own, if you like. Artistic talent is not a requirement, just make sure your dog faces have a nose, two eyes, two ears, and maybe a tongue or teeth as well.

Cut the pictures into their various component facial parts — one eye, one ear, the nose, and so on. These pieces will be small; to make them easier to handle, you could mount them on three by five cards.

Give each participant one facial feature. Their task is to assemble a complete dog face by finding other people holding the required pieces. Designate a place, maybe in the middle of each table, for the group so formed to display its dog face.

You can require all facial features in the final assemblage be from the same original dog face picture. Or, you can require only that each dog face have the usual supply of features, and see what kinds of mixed breeds appear.

Web

Checklist

Group size: up to about 20

Advance preparation: none

Materials: a large ball of string

Gather together and stand in a circle. Ask participants to think about who among the present company they rely on for various things having to do with the group's purpose, or for more personal needs. Explain that they will use the ball of string to make a representation of these connections.

Hand the ball of string to Mary, and she starts. Holding the loose end, she throws the ball of string to Ed, saying that she depends on him to make a pot of coffee for each meeting. Ed grasps the string, keeping the piece between him and Mary fairly taut, and throws the ball over to Cynthia, explaining that he counts on her to know and pass on the daily weather report.

Cynthia keeps the piece of string taut between her and Ed, and throws the ball to Randy, whose sense of humor she relies on to keep things in perspective. Randy passes to Colleen, who understands the copy machine's quirks and moods. Colleen passes to Shirley, who knows whose birthday is coming up. And so on. Continue for about five minutes, or until the group runs out of connections.

For the activity to be successful, everyone must be included at least once. Some people may find themselves holding several lengths of string, depending on the roles they play. The end product — a complex and interconnected web — will demonstrate visually the nature of the group's relationships.

Line-Up

You could start this activity by quoting former New York Yankees manager Yogi Berra, who once supposedly told his team to "line up alphabetically by height." (He also once instructed them to "pair up in threes.")

Explain that you want to experiment with different ways of lining up in order, to see which is most efficient. Instruct participants to work together to accomplish each line-up as quickly as possible, and then give a signal when they have achieved the proper order. If you have more than one team of about fifteen people, make it a competition among them.

SOME WAYS TO LINE UP:

Line up by age.

Line up by house number.

Line up by length of time of service to the organization.

Line up alphabetically by pet's names, or oldest child's names, or middle names, or names of home towns.

Line up by shoe size.

None of these, of course, is an efficient way to line up in order, but all are fun to try. They provide a way for participants to learn more

about each other, and the quick, purposeful, and possi
interaction required will help start conversations later.

Definitions

Checklist

Group size: any size; divide a large group into teams of
eight or less

Advance preparation: select several common words;
write out the dictionary definition but not the word itself

Materials: slips of paper containing the unidentified
definitions

Look through a dictionary, and choose four or five commonly used
words. Write out the definitions on slips of paper, one set of definitions for each team. Don't identify the words the definitions apply to.

FOR EXAMPLE:

"Any porous substance through which a liquid or gas is passed in
order to remove constituents such as suspended matter."

"A domesticated carnivorous mammal, raised in a variety of
breeds and probably originally derived from several wild
species."

"Lacking nothing essential to the whole; complete of its nature or
kind; in a state of undiminished or highest excellence; without
defect."

These words are, in order, filter, dog, and perfect.

Make your selections as easy or difficult as suits your purposes. If possible, choose words that apply in some way to the nature or purpose of your gathering. Teams will compete with each other to identify the definitions. The team with the most correct answers after two minutes wins.

Sayings

Checklist

Group size: any size, divided into teams of six to eight

Advance preparation: think of some common sayings; rewrite them, as described below

Materials: one list of the rewritten sayings for each team; pens or pencils

Most common sayings are easily understood, and their truth is clear, because they are brief, compact, and they use ordinary language. But consider these sayings, which have been brutally rewritten:

Avoid disposing of objects or resources that might at some time in the future be useful, or you will be unable to satisfy your potential desire to have these objects or resources at that time.

A boulder in motion provides an inhospitable environment for the growth of primitive vegetation.

Avoid divulging classified information in my presence, and I will avoid fabricating misinformation, falsehood, or prevarication to pass on to you.

Avoid disturbing a member of the species canis domesticus when it appears to be in a state of repose.

Under no circumstances allow an individual who appears to be gullible or vulnerable in some way to have an ordinary opportunity for a satisfactory outcome.

Alter or add to this list as you see fit, and give one copy to each small group. Group members must, as quickly as possible, translate these sayings back to their pithy, readable form. The translations are as follows:

Waste not, want not.

A rolling stone gathers no moss.

Tell me no secrets, I'll tell you no lies.

Let sleeping dogs lie.

Never give a sucker an even break.

Decide

Checklist

Group size: any size, working in pairs or groups of three

Advance preparation: think of a decision facing your group, or make one up

Materials: paper and pencils for each small group

Decisions are generally made by weighing pros and cons. The more difficult the decision, the more evenly balanced the pros and cons. The task in this activity is to virtually preclude a decision by coming up with pros perfectly counterbalanced by cons.

Present the group with a dilemma. It could be an actual decision currently facing your organization: should we expand our space, move to a new location, change our logo, take on new members, increase our public visibility, accept a donation from someone whose motives are suspect?

Or, it could be a completely fictional situation: should Heather and Wolfgang break up, get married, have a child, sell their car, move to Venice? In this case, creating a decision-making impasse will involve making up a little story about Heather and Wolfgang, who perhaps met when their carts collided in the super market candy and chips aisle.

To start out, provide one pro and one con. Should Heather and Wolfgang break up? They can never agree on a restaurant; they dance together beautifully. Each group then lists as many pairs of pros and cons as it can within five minutes. The group with the longest list wins.

Connections

Checklist

Group size: up to about thirty

Advance preparation: none

Materials: chalk board, or another medium that every one can see

Ask the group to come up with ten nouns, and write them in a column on the left side of the board. Then, ask for ten more nouns, and write them in a column on the right side of the board. Both of these lists are random, and have nothing to do with each other. Leave room for three columns in between them.

Let's say that the first word in the left hand column is coffee, and the first word in the right hand column is spotlight. The group must connect them by filling in three words in between. Each must relate to the word in the column immediately preceding it, but need not relate to the word in the left hand column:

coffee   morning   day   sunshine   spotlight

On the second line, maybe we have bread in the left hand column, and rabbit in the right hand column:

bread   wheat   farm   animal   rabbit

Move down the rows quickly, and continue until all ten are filled in.

Chapter
2

ICEBREAKERS AS INTRODUCTIONS

Simple and Spontaneous / 44

With a Little Prior Planning / 51

Planned in Advance / 61

• •

Meeting new people is surely one of life's greatest pleasures — under the right circumstances. Unfortunately, circumstances rarely seem to suit us exactly, and many of us find ourselves uncomfortable with people we don't know. If the occasion is an elevator ride from the first to the twenty-third floor, or a plane trip from Chicago to Dallas, a minimal level of common courtesy will see us through. But if we must work with the people we don't know, or plan with them, learn with them, teach them, make decisions with them, play with them, celebrate with them, have dinner with them, or carry on any aspect of life's nearly limitless opportunities with them, we want a way to feel more comfortable quickly.

That's where icebreakers as introductions come in. They are techniques meant to involve everyone present, bring a smile or two, and change each person's focus away from his or her discomfort and towards other members of the group and the reason for being together. Some activities involve little more than an elaborate exchange of names. Many in this chapter involve purposeful mingling — people moving around the room and talking to each other, with a common goal. The shared agenda immediately creates a sense of camaraderie, and it makes it easier for people to approach others, share a brief interaction, and move on to meet someone else.

The purpose of icebreakers as introductions is to allow people to establish some familiarity and common ground right away. Once we can relax together, especially if we've shared a laugh, we can more easily move ahead with work or play together.

Simple and Spontaneous

These require little or no prior planning, and only the simplest of props or materials, to be successful. You can launch into them at a moment's notice. They work with large or small groups, and take as much or as little time as you like.

Names

Checklist

Group size: any size, in groups of about 20 or less

Advance preparation: none

Materials: none

Time frame: short to medium, depending on group size and number of variations used.

Taking turns, each person says his or her first name, and adds a self-descriptive adjective that starts with the same letter as the name: Normal Nan, Judicious Jacob, Go-fo-broke Gary. For variety, add the adjective at the end: Andy the Adventurous, Nate the Nimble-witted.

If the group has a theme — a neighborhood planning group, for example — use that theme in coming up with adjectives: Streetlight Sue, Pothole Pete, Development Dan.

If you want to take the time, have each person repeat the adjectives and names of all the previous people before saying his or her own name. Depending on the nature of the group or the tone you want to set, provide help and encouragement as needed, or let each person flounder as the list gets longer.

Go around again, and again, as many times as seems useful or fun, using one or all of the following, or coming up with your own:

Occupations: These might be realistic — Linda the Librarian, Ed the Editor, or fanciful —Nate the Nightrider, Gary the Golf Pro.

Possessions: Real or desired — Dorrie's Desk, Jake's Jaguar, Harley's Harley.

Actions: Nora Notices Things, Jeff Joins Others, Ann Answers Questions, Pete Plays Hard.

Place names: Real — Chuck from Chicago; or fictional — Marion from Middle Earth.

Animal, flower, or tree names: Paula Pony, Lou Lilac Bush, Owen Oak Tree.

Try for as many combinations as you can: Friendly Fred the Financier Flies in from Frankfurt.

Have each person say the name of the person on his or her right, with any alliterative descriptor that has not yet been used.

By the end, the descriptors and phrases may bear only the most tenuous relationship to reality, but the process will reveal quite a bit about the personalities of those present, and no one will have trouble remembering names.

Circles

Checklist

Group size: any size

Advance preparation: none

Materials: none

Time frame: short to medium, depending on group size.

Form two concentric circles, so that each person in the group is facing another person. Each person in the outer circle offers a brief introduction to his or her partner in the inner circle. The introduction should include the person's name and one or two facts pertinent to the nature of the group or the reason for gathering — "I work in marketing;" "I know the bride from medical school;" "my son is the one who wouldn't share his markers;" "I live near the park on Oak Street and I'm concerned about the proposed highway expansion." The person in the inner circle then reciprocates.

When these introductions are complete, each person moves to the right, causing the circles to move in opposite directions and each person to have a new partner. Starting again with those in the outer circle, repeat the introductions. Participants may repeat the same pertinent fact with each new partner, or come up with something new each time. Continue until the circles return to their original positions, and the same people are facing each other as at the beginning.

Everyone in the outer circle has now met everyone in the inner circle, but those in each circle have not met each other. This level of familiarity may be sufficient for the group's purposes. If not, remedy the situation by allowing time for mingling, or by asking each person to introduce two people he or she has met who have not met each other.

Possessions

Checklist

Group size: any size, in groups of about 20 or less

Advance preparation: none

Materials: none

Time frame: short to medium depending on group size

Ask each participant to choose an object in his or her possession. It may be something dug out of a purse, briefcase, pocket, notebook, backpack, or satchel. It may be an article of clothing or jewelry, but it must be something the person is willing to part with momentarily.

Collect all the objects in the middle of the circle. One person starts by choosing an object which belongs to someone else. After identifying the owner, the person returns the object to him or her. Identifying the owner may be easy or difficult. If, after three or four false attempts to return the object the rightful owner has not been found, he or she should speak up and claim the object.

The owner then tells his or her name, and offers a brief explanation of what the object is, what importance or relevance it has, if any, and why it is in his or her possession at this event. He or she then chooses another object from the pile in the middle, and returns it to its owner, who provides the same introduction.

Continue until all the objects have been returned to their owners, and everyone has been introduced.

Squares

Checklist

Group size: any size, in groups of about 20 or less

Advance preparation: none

Materials: a role of toilet paper, or several roles for a very large group

Time frame: medium to long, depending on group size

Stand or sit in a circle, and pass the role of toilet paper around. Ask the participants to tear off as many squares as they like, but offer no explanation as to what the squares will be used for.

Once the role of toilet paper has made it all the way around, the introductions can begin. Taking turns, participants stand, or step inside the circle. After saying their names, they must tell one thing about themselves for each square of toilet paper they tore off.

They can reveal anything they like — age, address, phone number, marital status, number of children, place of employment, nature of job, what time they went to bed last night, greatest fear, most embarrassing moment, hopes and dreams for the future, how sleepy or alert they are at the moment — anything.

One fact counts for only one square, even if it is a complex fact. For example: "I had cereal for breakfast this morning. Also coffee. I had bananas slices on my cereal. And raisins. I read the paper while I ate." This revelation is worth one square, not five.

On the other hand, if, due to a fit of greed or an underlying pack-rat nature, someone tore off half the role, a limit could be placed on how much that person would say, or on how long he or she would have the floor.

Continue until everyone has been introduced, and all the squares accounted for and properly disposed of.

Ball

Checklist

Group size: any size, in groups of about 20 or less

Advance preparation: none

Materials: one or more balls of any size or description; inflated balloons work as well, or any object that can be easily and safely thrown and caught.

Time frame: short to medium, depending on group size

Stand in a circle. Go around once, each person stating his or her first name.

One person then throws the ball to someone else whose name he or she remembers. If Nate starts, for example, and if he remembers that the person directly across from him in the circle is Jacob, he will say "Nate to Jacob," and throw the ball to Jacob. Jacob might remember that the person next to him is Nan. He says "Jacob to Nan," and tosses the ball to her. Nan recalls Gary's name, says "Nan to Gary," and throws the ball to him. And so on. Participants may help those who are unable to remember any names at first. Continue until everyone has caught and thrown the ball at least twice.

For more fun, add more balls: in quick succession, for example, Nate throws a ball to Jacob, one to Nan, and one to Gary, saying his own name and the name of the person he is throwing to; each of those people quickly throws the ball to someone else, still calling out names, and pretty soon balls and names are flying so fast it will be difficult to keep up.

Once the names seem pretty familiar, add a competitive feature: anyone who drops a ball, or who misses a name, is out. Stop when almost everyone has been eliminated, or when a pre-announced time limit is up.

With a Little Prior Planning

These activities require just a little forethought and some easily prepared materials. Be creative in using them; adapt the materials to your own tastes and to the needs and nature of your gathering.

Partners

Checklist

Group size: any size

Advance preparation: create handouts containing a list of interview questions

Materials: the prepared handout, pens or pencils

Time frame: medium; depends on group size

Make sure that each person has the interview questions handout and a pen or pencil. Separate the group into pairs by numbering off one-two-one-two, by self selection, by random assignment, or by any method of your choice.

Allow five to ten minutes for the partners to interview each other, responding to the questions on the interview handout.

Examples of interview questions follow, but feel free to make up your own. Use as few or as many as you like. The questions can be ordinary and straightforward, meant only to impart necessary information, or they can be amusing or even risqué, meant to entertain as well. In any case, they can be tied in some way to nature or purpose of the gathering.

Alternatively, provide participants with blank paper instead of prepared questions, and leave the interview entirely to them. The process will require creativity, and the results will be unpredictable, which may be exactly what the group needs.

When the allotted time for interviewing is up, gather the group together again. Each participant will introduce his or her partner to the group as a whole, using the information gathered during the interview.

The interview should include, at minimum, each person's name and two or three things related to the nature of the gathering or the reasons for being there. Beyond that, here are some possible interview questions. Adding Why? to any or all of them would add depth to the interview.

> Favorites — food, restaurant, color, sport, flower, clothing style, song, movie, book, opera, play, entertainer, free-time activity, form of exercise, animal, type of vacation, city, form of architecture, type of art, type of music, and on and on.

> If you could be any place in the world, except here, right now, where would it be?

> Who, living or dead but not fictional, do you admire most?

> What makes you sad?

> What makes you laugh?

> If you could have dinner with any fictional character (not an author or actor) from any book, movie, or play, who would it be?

> If you had to identify yourself as an animal, what animal would it be?

> What is your ideal career; and are you in it?

> When you were a child, what did you want to be when you grew up?

> Name five things that are on your bedside table at home right now.

Describe exactly what you did before you arrived here today, starting with getting up this morning.

When was the last time you did something you really enjoyed, and what was it?

If you had control of your city's (or county's, or state's) budget, how would you spend it?

Pairs

Checklist

Group size: medium to large

Advance preparation: stick-on name tags as described below

Materials: prepared name tags

Time frame: medium to long, depending on group size

Prepare ahead by thinking of commonly used pairs of words. You will need one pair of words for each two guests or participants expected.

They could be pairs of things: salt and pepper, cup and saucer, sugar and spice, nuts and bolts, beer and peanuts, champagne and caviar, pen and paper, lock and key, knife and fork, surf and sand, ham and eggs, meat and potatoes, nickel and dime, flora and fauna, cat and mouse, dogs and cats, horse and rider, stocks and bonds, friends and neighbors, hill and dale, sun and moon.

They could be ideas: safe and sound, far and near, one and all, wild and woolly, right and wrong, up and down, power and glory, fame and fortune, straight and narrow, crime and punishment, pain and suffering, day and night, thick and thin, better and worse, clean and sober, high and dry, fast and furious.

They could be actions: come and go, hunt and fish, catch and release, buy and sell, rise and shine, ebb and flow, scrimp and save, song and dance, draw and paint, rock and roll.

They could be famous couples: Laurel and Hardy, Popeye and Olive Oyl, Simon and Garfinckle, Batman and Robin, Adam and Eve, Ernie and Bert, Sampson and Delilah, Dumb and Dumber, Tweedledee and Tweedledum, Lancelot and Guinevere, Tristan and Isolde, Chip and Dale, Mickey and Minnie, Rhett and Scarlett, Bill and Hillary, Jack and Jackie, George and Martha, Tom and Huck, Sammy Sosa and Mark McGuire, Ralph Kramden and Ed Norton, Han Solo and Princess Leia, Harry and David, Ben and Jerry.

They could be cities and states or countries: Akron, Ohio; Buffalo, New York; Sacramento, California; Reykjavik, Iceland.

They could even be separated parts of long words: sen/sibility, rene/gade, salmon/ella, poli/tician, metro/politan, retro/grade, super/visor, meti/culous, member/ship.

Prepare a stick-on name tag for each expected person by writing the person's name on the top half of the tag, and one word of a word pair on the bottom half.

A typical name tag might say "Doris" on the top, and "song" on the bottom. After being handed her name tag as she enters the gathering, and attaching it in a visible place on her person, Doris must search among all the other people present for the one whose name tag says "dance" on the bottom. This person is, of course, searching for her as well. Continue until all the pairs have located each other.

Mingling in a purposeful, rather than a random, way, helps assure that no one will feel left out, and allows the group to become acquainted quickly and comfortably.

Puzzles

Checklist

Group size: any size

Advance preparation: make jigsaw puzzles, as described below

Materials: pre-made puzzle pieces, one piece for each person

Time frame: medium

Prepare ahead by making several jigsaw puzzles. The number of puzzles you need will depend on the number of participants you are expecting. Each puzzle will be cut into six to eight pieces, and each participant will receive one piece.

To make your puzzles, cut pictures from magazines, catalogues, calendars, posters, wrapping paper, or any other source you can find. Choose the pictures based purely on their aesthetic or comic value, or choose them based on the theme or purpose of your get-together.

Mount each picture on light-weight poster board. All should be approximately the same size, and they should be large enough that, when cut, the resulting pieces will be easy to handle. Cut each mounted picture into six or eight jigsaw-like pieces.

Shuffle the pieces together, and hand them out randomly as participants enter the gathering. Once most people have arrived, instruct them to search for others holding pieces to their puzzles. When two people find that they have pieces of the same puzzle, they can band together looking for the others, or, in the interests of greater efficiency, they can split up, as long as they don't lose track of each other.

Designate a place for completed puzzles to be displayed. A group that succeeds in locating all its puzzle pieces and recreating the picture should offer a signal to the gathering that it has done so. If you like, give a prize to the first group to assemble its puzzle.

Purposeful mingling can help reduce the awkward feelings that many people experience when they come into a room full of strangers. It allows for laughter, light conversation, and a positive start to the gathering.

Actions

Checklist

Group size: up to about 25 or 30

Advance preparation: numbered name tags; worksheet handouts, as described below

Materials: numbered name tags, worksheet handouts, pencils

Time frame: short to medium; speed up the action, and the fun, by imposing a time limit

Number stick-on name tags from one up to the number of participants — one through twenty-five, if twenty-five people are expected. Prepare an Actions worksheet; an example follows, but please feel free to add to it, subtract from it, or make up your own altogether. Have enough copies for one per participant.

As people enter the gathering, hand them a pencil, a numbered name tag, and a worksheet. They attach the numbered name tag in a visible place, and start the worksheet by writing the number on the name tag on its top line. They fill in the remaining lines with the rest of the numbers, in order. The person with the name tag bearing number 18, for instance, in a group of twenty, will have 18 on the top line, then 19, 20, 1, 2, 3, and so on.

Participants must then find the person in the room wearing each number, and work through the prescribed actions on the worksheet, not necessarily in order. They check off each action after doing it. Continue until all worksheets are complete, or until a pre-announced time limit has been reached. If you impose a time limit, consider a prize or reward for the person whose worksheet is most complete.

Some of the suggested behaviors may not exactly come naturally to all those present. But, because everyone is performing the various actions at the same time, no one is likely to feel too silly, and a level of interpersonal comfort can be quickly achieved.

ACTIONS WORKSHEET

Your number is ____ .

Thumb wrestle with ____ .

Tweak ____'s nose.

Pat ____ on the top of the head.

Tell ____ your job is freelance assassin.

Make a face at ____ .

Sneak up behind ____ , cover his or her eyes, and say "Guess who?"

Tell ____ a knock-knock joke.

Straighten ____'s collar, tie, or scarf.

Imitate an animal for ____ .

Whisper in ____ 's ear.

Hop up and down while greeting ____ .

Compare your height to ____'s.

Link arms with ____ .

Smile silently at ____ .

Secretly hand any object of your choice to ____ .

Wave your arms like a windmill in front of ____ .

Ask ____ to dance.

Bring ____ a refreshment.

Hug ____ .

Take ____ by the hand....

....lead him or her to ____ .

Tell ____ your name is Ralph Waldo Emerson.

Brush imaginary crumbs off ____'s shoulder.

Greet ____ as though he or she were a long-lost childhood friend.

Tell ____ your birth date.

Don't smile at ____ .

Address ____ as John Jacob Jingleheimer Smith.

Give ____ a compliment.

Introduce yourself to ____ .

Categories

Checklist

Group size: any size

Advance preparation: prepare a categories question-naire; an example follows, but try to make yours relevant to the nature or purpose of your gathering. Leave room under each category for participants to write in the names of those who fit it. Have one copy for each partic-ipant.

Materials: prepared questionnaire, pens or pencils

Time frame: short to medium, depending on group size

Make sure that each person has a questionnaire and a pen or pen-cil. They must circulate among themselves, looking for people who fit the various categories on the questionnaire, and then list the names of those they find under that category.

Some categories will be obvious; if the questionnaire asks for all those who are wearing blue jeans, or all those who have brown eyes, simple observation will be enough, together with an exchange of names. Others could be more difficult to ascertain, and might require a short interview, or a request for a performance or demonstration.

Choose categories carefully; asking for all those with a receding hairline might be good for a laugh in some groups, but a sensitive issue in others. Asking for all those who are single or divorced might serve a useful purpose in some groups, but seem intrusive in others.

Continue until everyone has completed the questionnaire, or set a time limit and reward the person with the most complete questionnaire.

CATEGORIES QUESTIONNAIRE

Find everyone in the room who . . .

. . . . speaks more than one language.

. . . . has more than one dog.

. . . . is wearing athletic shoes.

. . . . is an only child.

. . . . was up until midnight or later last night.

. . . . can play Canasta.

. . . . can sing the Star-Spangled Banner.

. . . . can wiggle his or her ears.

. . . . has taken classes in drawing and painting.

. . . . plays a musical instrument.

. . . . is over fifty (or under 21).

. . . . has never gotten a traffic ticket.

. . . . is from Brooklyn.

. . . . has a tattoo.

. . . . drives a convertible.

. . . . exercises daily.

. . . . can name all cities with major league baseball teams.

. . . . has been to Paris.

. . . . is wearing just one earring.

. . . . is wearing red.

. . . . has four or more children.

. . . . scuba dives.

. . . . once owned a hula-hoop.

Planned in Advance

These require a little more planning a little further in advance, on the part of group leaders and participants. But, with the planning in place, they are easy to carry out, and they provide interesting and active ways for people to meet each other in groups.

Secrets

Checklist

Group size: any size

Advance preparation: before the gathering, ask all participants to submit a fact about themselves that others are unlikely to know, or that may be difficult to believe; prepare a list of these facts, without identifying their source.

Materials: handouts consisting of the list of facts about the people present, pencils or pens

Time frame: medium to long

Make it easy for people to submit their facts by including a blank for that purpose on a registration or RSVP form, with a brief explanation of the purpose. Make every effort to have a contribution from each person ahead of time, even if that means a few telephone calls or e-mail messages to those who are a little slow about responding.

You have no idea what little-known or hard-to-believe facts you will get. Maybe someone shook Bill Clinton's hand in Italy, someone else has a pilot's license, and a third person was an extra in *"Austin Powers."* On a dare, someone once accepted a motorcycle ride at dawn up the coast highway with a Hell's Angel. Someone else *was* a Hell's Angel.

Someone earned a black belt in karate at the age of nine. Another person performs stand-up comedy, and another tutors refugees.

List the various statements in no particular order on a sheet of paper, with a blank next to each one. Have enough copies for each participant and hand them out, with a pen or pencil, as people enter the gathering.

The task is for each person to discover and fill in the name that belongs with each statement. Doing so will require an interview which may be brief, but must be thorough enough to get the necessary information.

Direct questions are acceptable: "Are you the one who trains dolphins?" "Are you a marathon runner?" A less direct approach is also acceptable: "You look benevolent, like the sort of person who might have worked with Mother Theresa." In responding to questions, participants should not be coy or devious, but neither should they voluntarily divulge information without being asked.

Let the activity go on until everyone has completed every item. Or, set a time limit and award a prize to the person who made the most connections. In any case, purposeful mingling allows participants to get to know each other, and to move from person to person throughout the room, without the awkward silences and stilted conversations that can otherwise characterize groups of strangers.

Cartoons

Checklist

Group size: any size, more fun with more people

Advance preparation: collect cartoons from magazines and newspapers; these should all be of the same format: the drawing in a box and the caption underneath. You need one cartoon for every two expected participants. Cut off the captions, and mount caption and drawing separately on pieces of heavy paper or cardboard. Enlarging them first would make them easier to use.

Materials: mounted cartoon captions and drawings

Time frame: short to medium, depending on group size

In collecting the cartoons ahead of time, look for those that have some relevance to your group or function. Also look for those that are a bit subtle, or might require a little thought, or have a meaning that is not immediately evident, or have a drawing that could fit with any number of captions; in other words, don't make the task of matching them too easy. If you would like to use a cartoon with no caption, mount a strip of blank paper as the match for it.

As participants enter the gathering, hand each a cartoon drawing or a caption. The task for each person is to find the one other person in the room who holds the correct match to his or her drawing or caption.

For some, this will happen quickly and easily, but they must still check with several people before they can be sure they have the correct match. For others, especially those holding somewhat ambiguous drawings or obscure captions, the process will be longer and more difficult. As people make their way around the room, they should exchange names and brief introductory information with each other.

Provide wall space and tape, or a bulletin board, so that as people match their cartoons and captions they can display them together for everyone to enjoy. Continue until all participants have found the correct match. Or set a time limit, and at the end of it allow everyone to help those who are still looking. This activity provides another opportunity for purposeful mingling, as well as a chance to laugh together, and an easy way to meet and talk to others.

Babies

Checklist

Group size: up to about thirty people

Advance preparation: Ask each participant to bring to the gathering a picture of himself or herself as a baby or young child. Use Post-it Notes, or some other method that won't damage the pictures, to assign a number to each one. Display them with no identification other than the number.

Materials: sheet of paper numbered like the pictures, pencils.

Time frame: short to medium

Some of the pictures that people bring in will be tiny snapshots, perhaps damaged from time and wear. Others will be nicely framed portraits, preserved to last for generations. Plan a large enough display space to accommodate all of them. Keep in mind that every picture is extremely valuable to its owner, and take care that all are returned at the end of the activity in the same condition in which they arrived.

Some people may not have a picture of themselves as babies or children. Acceptable substitutes would include a picture of parents, siblings, children, other relatives, or ancestors. In these cases, supply this information in the display, without identifying the picture's owner. If picture number three, for example, is not the owner as a baby, but the owner's mother, the number tag should say Number 3; mother. Someone who forgot a picture might have one of a family member stuck away in a purse or wallet.

Collect the pictures as people enter, and hand out the numbered sheets of paper and pencils. Once all the pictures are included in the display, the task is for each participant to match the baby pictures with the people present, and fill in the appropriate name next to that number on the sheet. Doing so will require purposeful mingling, which will include close scrutiny of each other's facial features, as well as conversation.

If your group is small enough, sit together in a circle and hold the pictures up or pass them around. Work with each other to identify the owner of each one.

Alternatively, ask for pictures from some aspect of life that fits with the nature or purpose of your group or gathering — pets, homes, gardens, furniture, art, flowers, favorite neighborhood spots, vacations, hobbies, crafts, sports. These pictures could be personal, or they could be photographs cut from magazines or newspapers. Identifying their owners will require more guess work and conversation, and less attention to features and appearance.

Continue until everyone has identified all the babies, or set a time limit and award a prize to the person who made the most matches. Finish by asking each person to hold up or stand next to his or her picture, and introduce himself or herself to the group as a whole.

Bags

Have extra grocery bags on hand for those who might have forgotten to bring something; ask them to find five items from a car, purse, pocket, or briefcase to put in their bag.

Divide into small groups of up to ten by means of place cards at tables, numbering off, random selection, or arbitrary assignment. Put all the grocery bags belonging to members of the small group into the middle. Even ordinary grocery bags can be distinctive in some way, but they should not be labeled and their ownership should not be obvious.

One group member should reach into a bag, not his or her own, and pull out an object. Group members pass it around, identify it, and maybe speculate as to its meaning or the reason for its presence. The owner then identifies himself or herself, and explains the object to the group.

A tennis ball pulled from Dave's bag, for instance, might be perfectly obvious and straightforward: Dave enjoys playing tennis. Or, its significance might be a little more obscure: Dave's dog likes to play fetch with the tennis ball. Or, it could have a different meaning altogether: Dave feels like a tennis ball being hit back and forth between conflicting obligations. Dave should confirm any applicable interpretation the group comes up with, and complete the explanation if they leave anything out.

Take turns pulling objects out of bags, and continue until all the objects have been revealed and discussed. By this time, group members will have a pretty good idea what is important to each other, and will know a little about each other's personalities and lives.

In the interests of saving time, ask for fewer objects; even a single item of particular significance could help people get to know each other.

Instructions

Checklist

Group size: any size

Advance preparation: Devise instructions as described below, send them to participants several days prior to the event.

Materials: none

Time frame: short

You need at least two different instructions, so half the group will be told one thing and the other half something different. Examples follow, but please do not be bound by them. Your instructions should match the tone you want to set for your gathering, and should be as wild and outlandish or as simple and ordinary as you think appropriate.

Be careful, though, not to go too far. If you instruct some members of the group to wear costumes, and someone goes all out and dresses as Godzilla, he or she will not be happy to find other people not wearing costumes at all.

You can use as many instructions as you like, but make sure that at least three people are given the same instruction so everyone will have others to connect with. Communicate the instructions by mail, phone, or e-mail to participants several days ahead of time. Give the impression that this is important, and that everyone is being told the same thing.

On arrival, most participants will see right away that they were duped. But as long as they see that others were also duped, as long as the ruse didn't require too much effort on their parts, and as long as they are greeted in a spirit of lighthearted fun, it can be an occasion for laughter and not for hard feelings. Those who were given the same set of instructions are likely to recognize and gravitate towards each other, forming a good basis for introductions and getting acquainted.

SOME IDEAS FOR INSTRUCTIONS TO GIVE:

Due to lighting problems in the room we will be using, all participants are asked to wear a hat with a wide brim to protect their eyes.

The building management has informed us of a problem with leaking pipes in the ceiling of the room we will be using; please bring an umbrella.

Semi-formal attire requested.

Please come prepared to play a little basketball during breaks.

The theme for this event is a Hawaiian Luau; a prize will be given for the brightest, loudest Hawaiian shirt.

Our guest of honor is currently experiencing vision sensitivity and requests that guests avoid wearing bright colors; black would be ideal.

A great deal of material will be handed out during this event; please bring a laundry basket.

All participants are asked to contribute a large balloon to the celebration.

Chapter

3

ICEBREAKERS FOR EVENTS

Building Relationships / 72

Exploring Relationships / 81

Exploring Together / 89

. . . .

Parties and conventions, retreats and mixers, seminars and annual meetings; installing new officers, welcoming new members, sending retirees on their way; learning new methods, meeting the experts in the field, examining goals and directions — special events are an important aspect of the life of any organization. All such events present opportunities for group members to connect with each other, and to reaffirm or reexamine a connection to the organization.

Well placed icebreakers can help the event flow smoothly, and help carry out the interpersonal tasks associated with it. Bring together the more experienced and the less experienced group members, so they can talk to and learn from each other. Introduce the new panel of officers or the out-of-town experts in a way that allows for personal interaction with everyone.

Use icebreakers for networking, for exploring personal backgrounds and group priorities, for help in discussing ideas about the organization and attitudes about its purposes. If that sounds like heavy going, remember that the purpose of icebreakers is to put people at ease. They work to the extent that they are fast-moving, funny or surprising, and perhaps a bit irreverent. Their desired effect is like that of opening a window to a spring breeze or turning on the light in a dim room.

Building Relationships

Networking can be described as the art of connecting with other people in purposeful and mutually useful ways. In your group, it could mean helping a few newcomers meet everyone else, helping everyone else meet a few guests, or simply sharing important information among participants.

Hunt

Checklist

Group size: any size

Advance preparation: make a hunting list, as described below

Materials: hunting list, copies for all participants (except a select group), pencils or pens

Time frame: medium

This is like a scavenger hunt, except that participants are hunting not for objects, but for ideas, experiences, interesting facts, and colorful anecdotes from members of a special small group designated for that purpose.

Select your group of respondents; these are the people who will be responding to the scavenger hunt questions. Maybe they are new members, new officers, special guests, experts in the field, or honorees. Maybe they all have birthdays that month. Or maybe they are random choices. In any case, designate them with special name tags, hats, flowers, or colored ribbons.

Create a hunting list similar to the example below. If possible, make the items on your list meaningful to your organization, or to those who will be responding to them. If your group of respondents consists of new officers, for example, you could ask for one good idea, a new nick name for the group, or a color that describes the organization. Give everyone except the respondents a copy of the hunting list and a pencil.

Set a time limit, making sure it's long enough to complete the process, but not so long that people end up standing around with nothing to do; the ideal time frame will depend on the size of your group, the number of respondents, and the number of items on your hunting list.

Through purposeful mingling, participants seek out the respondents, and ask for the items on the list. They may check them off or write down the responses as they go. The goal is for each participant to complete the list with each respondent, but, in order to keep things moving, they may ask for only one item per interaction.

When the time limit is up, reconvene the group and ask participants to share the most interesting things they learned about the respondents.

SOME IDEAS FOR A HUNTING LIST:

Tell me . . .

. . . a childhood memory

. . . something that should be changed within the year

. . . something you own that you value highly

. . . a good day for you

. . . something that should never change

. . . how you spent your last vacation

. . . a source of joy

. . . the first names of three family members

. . . an unfulfilled desire

. . . an example of wasted effort

. . . your favorite food

. . . one hope you have

. . . an example of time well spent

. . . a constant frustration

. . . a good name for a pet

Press Conference

Checklist

Group size: any size, divided into groups of 5

Advance preparation: none

Materials: paper and pencils

Time frame: medium to long, depending on group size

This is another way to encourage interaction between a few — new members, visitors, officers, honored guests, experts, trainers, award winners, retirees — and the many. Begin by breaking the larger group into small groups of about five people. Each small group should have paper and pencils.

While the select few who will be respondents cool their heels and wait, the small groups should take five minutes to think of a few questions they want to ask each of them. The questions could be personal and idiosyncratic: What did you have for dinner last night? What books have you read recently? How's your golf game?

They could address burning issues of current interest: Who do you think will win the World Series? What future do you predict for airline food? Don't you agree that Samuel L. Jackson should have had a larger role in *Star Wars Episode I*?

Or the questions could have to do with the reason the respondents were singled out. New members, for instance, could be asked what brought them to the organization. New officers could be asked about their goals for the organization. Visiting experts could be asked about their backgrounds or points of view. Award winners could be asked what inspired them.

In any case, questions should be brief, they should allow for brief answers, and they should be about the respondents, not the organization, its membership, its direction, or the event itself. Such questions could be listed and addressed at another time.

When each small group has a list of three to five questions, the press conference can begin. Reconvene the large group, and arrange the chairs so that questioners face respondents. Just like a real press conference, participants raise their hands, wait to be recognized, and ask their questions.

Continue until a pre-announced time limit has been reached, until all questions have been asked, or until the momentum of the process seems to slow.

Stations

If you have five important people — visitors, experts, honorees, trainers, trainees, new officers, new members, or anyone else — that you want all participants to meet, you need five stations. If you have four, you need four stations, six, six stations, and so on.

Designate your stations in a way that relates to your organization, or to the particular people you want to introduce. For out-of town visitors, for example, have a station for the town or region that each is from. For specialists in the field, choose stations that represent the specialty. Or, choose from the list of examples that follows. Post a sign identifying each station, and decorate the area with pictures or symbols representing it.

SOME IDEAS FOR STATIONS:

Subway Stops: Wall Street, Canal Street, Grand Central, Times Square, Lincoln Center

Turnpike Exits: Monroeville, Breezewood, Carlisle, Morgantown, Levittown

European Cities: Stockholm, Luxembourg, Paris, Munich, Prague

Continents: Asia, Australia, South America, North America, Europe

Planets: Mercury, Venus, Mars, Saturn, Jupiter

Rooms: Kitchen, Dining Room, Bedroom, Family Room, Library

Baseball Teams: Yankees, Red Sox, Tigers, Cubs, Dodgers

Band instruments: Flute, Trumpet, Trombone, Tuba, Drum

Position each important person at a station, which will be his or her home base for the activity. Participants will move from station to station, giving each person a chance to meet and converse briefly with the guests. The station names and motifs provide conversation starters; they are entertaining, and they are also useful if they relate to your group or your guests.

Divide into as many small groups as you have stations, assign each small group a starting station, and ask them to move to the next station when they hear your signal. Continue until everyone has had a chance to visit every station.

Data

Checklist

Group size: any size

Advance preparation: think of what information you need or want from all participants

Materials: paper and pencils, markers, and newsprint posted throughout the room

Time frame: medium

At the beginning of an event, you might want to gather information in categories such as these: participants' needs or hopes for the event, their reasons for attending, their experience level with regard to the topic of the event, their attitudes or ideas about the purpose of the event, their preferred learning or interpersonal styles.

Towards the end of the event, you might want to gather data in categories such as these: participants' opinions as to the high point and the low point of the event, things they learned, things they might do differently as a result, ideas about improving the event, ideas for next year's event.

At any time, you can gather data in any set of categories you like: participants' home towns, their favorite vacation spots, their political perspectives, their hopes for the future, the worst mistake they've ever made, their opinions and ideas about various issues.

Once you have decided what kinds of data to collect, group the participants into teams. Assign one team to each category of information you have selected. Give them three minutes to devise a fast and effective method of collecting their assigned information from everyone present. They might come up with a couple of yes or no questions. They might assign each team member to interview a certain number of participants. They might decide on a sampling technique rather than trying to reach everyone. In any case, they will have only three minutes to carry out the task.

Ask the teams to start collecting data, using whatever strategies they came up with. Call time after three minutes. Give them another three minutes to process their data, and summarize it on a sheet of newsprint posted for that purpose. End the activity by asking each team to share what it learned with the group as a whole.

Clubs

Checklist

Group size: any size

Advance preparation: newsprint, blackboard, or overhead

Materials: paper and pencils, straight pins

Time frame: medium

Think of the various ways people categorize themselves, some by choice and some not:

Age, gender, race, ethnicity, religion, marital status, status with regard to parenthood, sexual orientation, birth order, family of origin, home town or region, physical characteristics, education, economic status, employment status, profession, beliefs, politics, preferences, interests, personality type, energy level, sleeping habits, food choices, style choices, recreational choices, status with regard to pet owner- ship, activities, memberships, and astrological signs, to name a few.

Ask the group to brainstorm a list of such categories, and examples of them:

physical characteristics: short person

sleeping habits: night person

activities: tennis player

personality type: introvert

place of origin: person from Illinois

Pass out paper, pencils, and pins. Ask participants to complete this sentence:

I'm a(n) ___ .

Then ask them to complete the same sentence ten times, with ten different endings. They should pin the resulting lists to their fronts, and begin purposefully mingling, with the goal of finding two other people as similar to themselves as possible, to form a "club."

Call time after a few minutes, and change the goal. This time, participants should look for two other people as different from themselves as possible, to form a new club. Depending on the nature of your group, one of these goals might be easier to accomplish than the other.

After a few more minutes, change the goal again. Ask all the short people, for instance, to come together. Then, ask all the people from Illinois to come together. Then, all the night people, all the introverts, all the people who play tennis, all the people who like rock and roll, all the lawyers, and so on, as long as you like. End by asking the entire group to reconvene, forming one big club.

A word of caution: if you are at the annual meeting of Bird Lovers of America, and you call for all the cat owners to come forward, you might bring out some strong feelings among the participants. Be sensitive to the nature of your organization, and be aware of the tone you want to set for your event.

Exploring Relationships

How well do members of your organization know each other? What do they think of each other? How do they interact with each other? Your event might provide the perfect opportunity to challenge interpersonal assumptions, to reshape relationships, and to shift the status quo. Have fun!

Lies

Checklist

Group size: any size, divided into small groups of up to ten

Advanced preparation: none

Materials: none

Time frame: short to medium, depending on the size of the small groups

Choose a method to determine who will start in each small group; maybe the person who most recently had a birthday, or the person who lives furthest away, or the person who has the broadest hand-span.

Once chosen, that person says three things to the group about him or herself. Two of these things must be true, and one must be a lie. The person should make every effort to confound those trying to figure out which is which.

The other group members then discuss among themselves which statements they believe to be true, and which they think is false. Once they have reached general agreement, the person who spoke comes clean. He or she clears up any misunderstanding, adds briefly to the true statements, discusses the lie and why it was or wasn't believable, and adds any relevant background information.

The person to his or her left then makes three statements, two true and one a lie, and the group responds as before. Continue until everyone has had a turn.

Groups who know each other well will be surprised how easily they can be duped by their companions. Those who are new to each other will be surprised how much information they can pick up from subtlety and nuance. In either case, participants are likely to learn something about themselves and about how they relate to each other.

Chance

Checklist

Group size: any size; break a large gathering into groups of 10 or 12

Advanced preparation: devise a list of chance questions

Materials: a pair of dice for each small group

Time frame: medium

In the first round of this game, each person roles the dice, and then answers a question from the list of chance questions. If you roll a six, you answer question number six.

In the second round, each person rolls a single die, and then answers questions from the list asked by group members. If you roll a four, the group may ask you four questions.

In the third round, each person rolls a single die, and then answers questions not yet answered. If you roll a three, you answer three questions that you haven't answered before.

In devising your list of twelve chance questions, consider the nature of your group, the goals of your event, the tone you want to set, how well participants know each other, and the amount of interpersonal risk you want them to take. Think about whether you want the game to be primarily for fun, or primarily to promote interpersonal growth, and make your questions lighthearted or incisive accordingly.

SOME SAMPLE QUESTIONS:

1. Describe in detail your daily routine.

2. What have you done in your life that was really stupid?

3. What aspect of your life are you proudest of?

4. What is your idea of a good time?

5. What is it about other people that most gets on your nerves?

6. What did you want to be when you grew up?

7. What do you like about traveling?

8. If you could choose one daily chore that you never had to do again, what would it be?

9. Describe the trait you possess that you most enjoy.

10. In what ways are you careless?

11. Describe the last thing you did that was really fun.

12. When you first meet someone, how do decide whether or not you like that person?

Rules

This is a two-phase activity. You can do either part, or both. Be sure to allow some time for discussion afterwards, since feelings are likely to run high.

PHASE ONE:

Announce that you are going to play a game, and hand out objects to play with. These can be anything fairly small and easy to handle: pennies, balls, stones, plastic cup-holders, buttons, scarves, small pillows. If your group is larger than about twenty, give one object to each group of four; otherwise, give each person an object.

Say that the game will start on the count of three, then count off and say go. Give no further instructions. When people ask what they are supposed to do, say "play!" Most participants will try to do so, but the pointlessness will quickly become obvious, as will players' frustration and annoyance. Arbitrarily declare a winner, and say that the game is over.

In response to the inevitable disgruntled muttering, ask what the problem is. Why didn't people like the game? It won't take long for the group to point out that a game with no rules makes no sense and is no fun.

Ask the group to devise some rules — to make up a game using the objects they have been given. Write the rules where everyone can see them, then start again, trying to play by the new rules.

If the rules are good, play until the game ends. Most likely, however, the group will find that the rules need some tweaking: they are unclear, or unfair, or impossible. Depending on how much time you want to spend, you could revise the rules until you have a fun and workable game. The point, however, is not creating a game, but experiencing the absence of rules, the presence of poor rules, and the difficulty of creating good rules. Finish with a brief discussion of what this experience was like.

PHASE TWO:

Divide into two teams, and form lines. Give each team an object of play. Explain that this is a relay race; the first team to pass the object from one end of the line to the other wins. Say one-two-three-go.

Stop play almost immediately after it starts: you forgot to mention that this is supposed to be a blind relay race, and participants must close their eyes.

After another brief interval, stop play again: you remembered that each person must turn around once before passing the object to the next person.

Interrupt several more times to add rules: players must pass the object over their left shoulders; receivers must face away from passers; passers must say the name of their receivers, and so on.

Finally, allow the race to finish; if your timing is good, this will be before the players mutiny. Finish with a brief discussion of the experience. If you have done both phases, compare them: no rules, too many rules; self-made rules, imposed rules; no guidelines, constant interruption. Ask participants to think about these experiences in light of their relationships with each other: did they feel drawn together in shared adversity, or annoyed with perceived ineptitude? In which situation were they more likely to work together and cooperate? Which situation made them feel more competitive with each other?

Spy

Checklist

Group size: at least 20

Advanced preparation: designate spies, and brief them as to their assignment

Materials: none

Time frame: medium

Designate one or two or more spies, depending on the size of your group, and brief them as to their mission. Do this in private and before the activity begins. Only you and the spies know who they are.

Assemble the group in a large open space, either indoors or out. Explain that dangerous terrorist spies have infiltrated the organization. Their goal is to bump off as many members as possible, in order to gain control of its vast resources of wealth and information. You can make up a story line that fits with your organization's history or purpose, or with the theme of your event.

The identity of the spies is unknown. Their modus operandi is unknown, except that they kill people by winking at them. No one is safe, and everyone must have a bodyguard.

Instruct participants to look around them and select a bodyguard. But caution them that the bodyguards' identities must also remain secret, even to them, otherwise they become ineffective. No one should reveal, by word or gesture, the bodyguard they have chosen. After bodyguards have been selected, explain that one must be within arm's distance of one's bodyguard to be protected.

Participants then begin moving around. The first goal is to get within arm's distance of one's chosen bodyguard without revealing his or her identity. The bodyguards, of course, are trying to stay close to their own bodyguards.

If a spy winks at someone who is not within arm's distance of his or her bodyguard at that moment, he or she must fall over dead. This depends on the honor system, since presumably no one but the victim knows that a wink occurred, or who the bodyguard in question is.

The second goal of the activity is to identify the spies. An accusation can be made at any time, by anyone other than a victim. If the accusation is false, the accuser leaves the game. If the accusation is correct, that spy is out of business. Play until all spies are identified.

Take a few minutes to discuss the relationship issues involved: unknown members of the group are dangerous in unknown ways; protection is available within the group, but it is anonymous and unreliable; trust is nonexistent. Ask participants if, and to what extent, they experience similar conditions in real life.

Stones

Checklist

Group size: up to about twenty

Advance preparation: gather or purchase small, attractive stones

Materials: one stone for each participant

Time frame: short to medium

This is an effective closing activity at the end of an event. If circumstances permit, precede it with a walk outdoors, in a park or nature center, along a creek, on a beach, through a meadow, or across the back yard. Ask participants to pick up a small stone, a shell, a pine cone, an acorn, or something else that attracts them, to use in the activity.

If the site of your event has no access to nature, you could ask participants to bring a stone or a shell with them, and drop it into a basket set out for that purpose. Or, supply the objects yourself. If you cannot collect things from nature, specialty and craft shops often sell attractive polished stones or shells inexpensively.

Ask participants to sit in a circle. Pass the basket containing the stones, and ask each person to take one. Then, one person starts by saying one thing he or she learned or changed or took from the gathering, and one thing he or she wants to leave to the gathering. You might have broadened your views regarding a group controversy, for instance, and you might want to leave the group with your favorite joke.

As each person finishes, everyone passes the stone they are holding to the person on their left, and receives a stone from the person on their right. The next person then says what he or she has to say.

By the time everyone has spoken, all the stones have been touched by everyone present, and each person has is or her own stone back. You could collect them in the basket again, and keep them for some future event. Or, you could allow participants to take their stones home, imbued with whatever meaning and memories they choose to give them.

To use this as an opening activity, ask people to introduce themselves as they pass the stones, and to say one or two things about themselves, or about their hopes or goals for the event. To use it as a mid-session activity, simply change the statements you ask for to suit your needs of the moment.

Exploring Together

Problems, puzzles, difficulties, uncertainties, and dilemmas all succumb more easily to group rather than individual efforts to resolve them. Try these activities to challenge your group, to help participants in your event work together, or simply to shake things up and have a good time. Each of these icebreakers is a team experience which requires the efforts of every team member to succeed.

Packing

Checklist

Group size: any size, divided into teams of five

Advance preparation: none

Materials: packing materials such as brown wrapping paper, packing tape, string, labels

Time frame: short

One person from each group of five must volunteer to be the package. This person should be a willing volunteer, ideally someone who isn't claustrophobic and who doesn't mind being manhandled a little, as gently as possible, of course.

Supply each group with enough packing materials to make a credible package of the volunteer, suitable for mailing or shipping, complete with destination label, return address, and postage — oh, and breathing holes. Allow no more than ten minutes to create the package.

Once each group has packaged its volunteer, compare the results. Rate the packages according to how neatly they are wrapped, how mailable they might be, and how pleasant or unpleasant the experience was for the volunteer. Award a prize to the winning team.

Since the volunteers might be pretty uncomfortable by that time, don't take too long to judge. Carefully unwrap the volunteers, help them up, dust them off, and congratulate each of them for being a good sport.

The idea of packing a person for mailing without benefit of a carton may strike participants as odd. The challenge is to complete the task gently but completely, with no injury to the person or dignity of the volunteer. Doing so requires thoughtful planning and coordinated efforts on the part of team members.

Escape

Checklist

Group size: up to about 20

Advance preparation: prepare a "pit," from which participants must escape

Materials: rope long enough to create a pit of the necessary size

Time frame: medium

The size of your pit will depend on the number of people in your group. If you have more than twenty people, divide into two teams, with two pits. In this case, you could make it a competition, with the team completing the task first winning.

Using your ingenuity and whatever materials you have at hand, enclose the "pit" with rope at about chest height. Everyone starts out in the pit. The group's task is to get everyone out. This is no easy matter, since participants may not go under the rope, nor may they touch it on their way over. Those who do must go back and try again. Participants may, however, make use of whatever it is that supports the rope and keeps it in place.

The plan must include escape for everyone; no one may be left behind. There are several possible means of escape, but no sure-fire, fool-proof method. Maybe those who are physically stronger can get out first, and then help the others. Or maybe the smallest people can be helped out first, and then work together to get the others out. Some rather close physical contact will almost certainly be necessary, involving lifting, climbing on, and otherwise touching each other.

The point of the activity is to experience the kind of interaction necessary to plan and attempt to carry out the escape; the success of the plan is secondary. If, however, after some time has elapsed and the group has made little progress, stop and try to figure out why. Is it a lack of ingenuity, trust in each other, or physical ability? Does the task seem too daunting? Or are participants simply convulsed with laughter, rendering them incapable of accomplishing the goal?

Rethink the strategy, and try again, but don't let the activity go on past the point of being entertaining or interesting. Take a few minutes at the end to talk about what worked and what didn't, what it was like to work together to free each other, and what it was like to succeed — or not.

Jewelry Store

Checklist

Group size: any size, divided into teams about five

Advance preparation: prepare a copy of the story and true/false statements for each team

Materials: the stories and statements, one answer sheet

Time frame: short

Ask each team to read the story about the jewelry store, and then mark each of the statements that follow it true or false.

THE STORY

A business person was about to lock up the jewelry store when a man holding a bag pushed his way in. He demanded that one of the jewelry cases be opened. The owner unlocked the jewelry case, and its contents were removed. A dog appeared and began barking. The man ran away.

TRUE OR FALSE?

1. The man pushed his way in before the owner locked the door.

2. The man was not carrying anything.

3. Someone took jewelry out of the case.

4. The story is about two people and a dog.

5. The store was protected by a guard dog.

6. The robber ran away.

7. The man demanded jewelry from the owner.

8. Someone unlocked the jewelry case.

Allow two minutes for the teams to respond to the statements. They must reach consensus, but not necessarily unanimous agreement. They must respond true or false to every item in order. They may not go back and change an earlier response. Reconvene the group as a whole to discuss the answers.

Good communication is often based on assumptions, and reasonable assumptions are based on context and past experience. But they're not always accurate. Ask what assumptions group members made, and whether or not they still seem like reasonable assumptions once they know the answers.

Answers:

1. False: the man pushed his way in before a business person locked the door.

2. False: the man was holding a bag.

3. False: the story does not say what was in the jewelry case.

4. False: it mentions three people — a business person, the owner, a man — and a dog.

5. False: the story doesn't mention the dog's purpose or where it came from.

6. False: the story doesn't mention a robber.

7. False: the man demanded that one of the cases be opened.

8. True: the owner unlocked it.

Time Bomb

Make a "time bomb" by partially filling a plastic beverage bottle with water, and replacing the cap. Attach a small timer or a watch with an alarm, set to go off when the specified time is up, about three to five minutes. Place the "bomb" inside an enclosure made by arranging four chairs in a square, and connecting them with a rope or cord.

Supply a variety of tools, such as rope or cord, coat hangers, kitchen utensils, knitting needles, claw hammers, bicycle locks, shoe horns, magnets, baskets or bowls, newspapers, screw drivers, and other items which may or may not be useful in extricating the bomb from its enclosure.

Using their ingenuity and any or all of the tools provided, each team must remove the bomb from the enclosure without stepping or reaching into it. They must do this within a specified time limit, three to five minutes.

Start by allowing the teams several minutes to hold planning sessions. During this time, they figure out a bomb removal method that all team members believe will work, and they choose the tools they want to use.

The team with the youngest member goes first. They do their best to get the bomb out before it explodes. Their turn is over when they succeed or when the timer goes off after three to five minutes.

Subsequent teams, of course, can learn from the experiences of those who went ahead of them, and they can talk about what they see, but they may not hold another planning session. If more than one team succeeds, the team that worked the fastest wins.

There is no single solution to this problem. Each team will go at it differently, and the teams might become quite competitive with each other. Even so, the experience of working with team mates to devise and carry out a solution is more important than the eventual outcome.

After all the teams have had a turn, allow time for a short, general discussion of what worked and what didn't. If you like, you can reward the most well conceived plan as well as the most expertly executed plan.

Target

Checklist

Group size: up to about twenty

Advance preparation: place a target on the ground, mark it with a flag or stick

Materials: blindfolds, a target, and a flag or stick

Time frame: medium

This is a two part activity. The first part involves trying to find the target working entirely alone and significantly impaired, and the second part involves trying to accomplish the same thing by working together as a group. It is an outdoor activity, meant to be carried out in a large open space, preferably a grassy field rather than a parking lot. For the target, use something flat and not too small. A compact disc case would do, or a box lid, or a wooden plate.

Ask participants to line up along a starting line, and place the target at a good distance from it, about thirty yards out. Mark the target with a flag or a stick, and ask participants to note closely its location in relation to their spot along the starting line. Then ask them to put on blindfolds. Remove the flag, but leave the target in place.

For the sake of safety, two or three people should not wear blindfolds in order to look out for everyone else. They are not searching for the target, but are watching to make sure no one trips or wanders off or bumps into anything. They have the authority to shout "stop" if the proceedings threaten to degenerate into chaos, and then everyone must stop and stand still until given the all-clear to move again.

Participants leave the starting line and move forward, approaching the target. Not only are they blindfolded, but they may not speak to each other, and they must do their best to avoid bumping into each other. Time is not a factor. Moving fast will not accomplish anything, and moving slowly will not be a disadvantage.

Participants get as close as they think they can to the target; they need not be on top of it or touching it. They then stand still, remove their blindfolds, and wait for everyone else to stop.

Ask everyone to look around, and assess the success or lack of success group members achieved. Take a few minutes to talk about strategies. Ask those who managed to get close to the target how they did it, and ask those who wandered far afield what they might do differently.

Return to the starting line for the second part of the activity. Replace the flag over the target, so participants can note its location again. Allow a few minutes to plan a strategy. This time, while participants must still wear blindfolds, they may talk to each other and even touch each other if they think that will help them find the target. Remove the flag, and get started.

The group is likely to locate the target in a matter of minutes. Effective strategies usually involving ongoing communication with each other and holding hands while moving down the field. If for some reason the group can't find the target, stop and rethink the strategy, and then try again.

Take a minute or two to compare the experiences of trying to find the target alone, and trying to find it as part of a group. Are there advantages and disadvantages both ways? Which was more challenging? Which was more fun?

Chapter

4

ICEBREAKERS FOR FUN

• •

The icebreakers in this chapter have no agenda and no expectation other than fun. They make no pretenses about seeking higher purposes, but aim only to provide an island of mirth in the middle of your gathering. Such an island, of course, is a wonderful thing to encounter in most gatherings, with the possible exception of funerals. Family reunions, wedding or baby showers, holiday parties, company picnics, retirement parties, and even more serious-minded gatherings such as retreats or conventions, can all benefit from a little pure fun.

Children are the masters of fun, and some of these icebreakers are variations on tried and true children's games, like musical chairs or tag or twister. While the only agenda is fun, many lend themselves to modifications that can help make them relevant to your event or your group. You can use them at the beginning or at the end of your gathering, but they may fit best somewhere in the middle. Use them to make a transition from one thing to another, to energize, or to shift gears.

One person's fun might be another person's tedium, so the key with these, as with all icebreakers, is to keep them short, keep the energy level high, and stop them before the momentum wears out. Some people like word games. Others like memory games or games that involve mental sparring with their fellow participants. Still others require intense physical activity for an experience to qualify as fun. And then there are those who crave silliness. This chapter contains a little something for everyone.

Playing with Words

Word games — with a couple of memory games thrown in — have probably been around since the first humans developed language. They usually require no materials other than creativity and ingenuity, and so can be played spontaneously any time, any place, within any time frame. Use them to fill the odd five minutes, or to help shift gears between agenda items.

Sentences

Checklist

Group size: any size

Advance preparation: none

Materials: paper and pencils

Time frame: varied

Starting with A, and working through the alphabet, participants write a complete sentence of at least five words, all of which start with the same letter. The sentence must contain a subject and a verb, and a few modifiers. Articles and prepositions need not start with the letter in question, but don't count towards the five required words. The sentences must make sense, of a sort, and the best will evoke a visual image. If your group is artistic, draw the pictures, too.

SOME EXAMPLES:

Ambitious acrobats ardently argued for arithmetic.

Bellicose ballplayers bellowed belligerent balderdash.

Excited editors educated enemy entertainers at the exit.

Querulous queens, in a quandary, quit quilting.

Alternatively, ask for complete sentences in which all words start with consecutive letters of the alphabet. In this case, articles and prepositions count toward the five-word requirement, and they must fit the pattern:

After bedtime, certain dogs eat fresh greens hungrily, in June.

Keeping low, men noticed open pens.

Quietly, returning soldiers traded under vegetable wagons.

Xylophonists yelled zealously about big cats.

You can make this an ongoing activity, spending a few minutes on it at several different times during your gathering. Make it a team or an individual activity. If you like, require that the sentences have something to do with your organization or your gathering. Ask for volunteers to read the sentences they have created. Or, post them where everyone will see them, and ask participants to put stickers on their favorites.

The Word

Checklist

Group size: any size, in small groups of about ten

Advanced preparation: none

Materials: none

Time frame: short

One person volunteers to leave the group. During his or her absence, the others decide on a word that they will try to get the volunteer to say on his or her return. The word could be anything at all, outlandish or risqué or nonsensical, or tied in some way to the nature of the gathering.

When the volunteer returns, after about a minute, group members have five minutes to induce him or her to say the word in question. They do this by engaging in conversation, drawing the volunteer in by means of questions and comments directed toward him or her, and attempting to steer the subject matter in the desired direction.

No one other than the volunteer may say the word or any form of it. No one may give direct clues. Synonyms and homonyms don't count, nor do forms of the word other than the one agreed upon.

Depending on the cleverness of those directing the conversation, and the astuteness of the volunteer, accomplishing the desired result may be harder than it seems. Laughter is likely to take over after a few minutes of frustrated efforts and close calls. When the group succeeds, or at the end of five minutes, ask for another volunteer and decide on a different word, or move on to something else.

Headlines

Checklist

Group size: any size, in small groups of five to eight

Advance preparation: none

Materials: paper and pencils

Time frame: short

Working together, the group members write a headline having to do with the occasion, the organization, its members, or themselves.

It could be entirely fanciful:

DRAGON INVADES HOLIDAY BASH — KNIGHTS PREVAIL

It could be factual, more or less:

HOLIDAY PARTY DRAWS BIG-TIME — KIDS INCLUDED

It could be hopeful:

KEY PLAYERS BACK DISPUTED "INSTANT HOLIDAY"

It could say anything group members want to say, with one catch. Each word in the headline must start with the first initial of someone in the group. (The group that came up with the examples included Dave, Inez, Helen, Brad, Kathy, and Paul.) No first letter may be used more than once, unless it occurs as a first initial in the group more than once.

Spend no more than five minutes writing the headlines, then have the groups take turns reading them. If you like, post them in a central place, along with the first names of the people who wrote them.

Six

> ## Checklist
>
> Group size: up to about thirty
>
> Advanced preparation: gather the six objects you want to use
>
> Materials: six objects, as described below; blindfolds for everyone; paper and pencils
>
> Time frame: short

Decide on six objects of varying size, shape, and consistency — maybe a potato, an unshelled walnut, a swatch of fake fur, a paint roller pad, a sandpaper cube, and a large carrot. If you like, you can include something that will feel gross, like a peeled grape or a piece of raw meat. Feathers, fringe, leather, beadwork, shells, ice cubes, a baggie filled with sand, and Silly Putty or some other gooey stuff you can buy at toy stores also make interesting textures.

Aim for mystery and maybe even disgust, but use common sense in your choice of objects. Avoid glass, raw eggs, or anything else that might break. Avoid sharp objects like knives, forks, screw drivers, pencils, or knitting needles. Gather the objects together and keep them out of sight.

Ask everyone to sit in a circle, and put on a blindfold. The blindfolds are unnecessary, by the way, if you can darken the room sufficiently so that no one can identify the objects except by touch.

One by one, pass the objects around the circle. Don't start the second one around until the first has made it back to you. Participants may handle the objects all they like before passing them on. But they should for the most part maintain silence, and not chatter among themselves about what each object is or how it feels. A few exclamations of surprise, recognition, or distaste are acceptable.

When all six of the objects have been all around the circle, and are again put away out of sight, participants may remove their blindfolds. They then write a list of the six objects in the proper order. Anyone who correctly identifies all objects and lists them properly is a winner. Depending on the objects you chose, providing napkins might be a thoughtful touch.

Tray

Checklist

Group size: any size

Advance preparation: assemble twenty to twenty-five things to put on a tray

Materials: a tray, things to put on it, a scarf to put over it, paper and pencils

Time frame: short

Your tray could contain objects that are related, such as tools, kitchen gadgets, small toys, office supplies, school supplies, foods, sports memorabilia, or board game pieces. The objects could be related in some way to the nature of your group or your gathering. A tray for a baby shower, for instance, could include diaper pins, rattles, small stuffed animals, little hats, pacifiers, and so on. Or, the objects could be completely unrelated and random — anything and everything.

Keep the tray covered with a scarf or towel. Hand out paper and pencils. Uncover the tray, and let everyone get a good look at it. No one may write while the tray is uncovered. After about a minute, cover the tray again.

Ask participants to list the items they saw on the tray. If the tray contains three nails, then a person who writes "nail" is less correct than the person who writes "three nails." Those who correctly remember the largest number of things are winners.

Lists

Checklist

Group size: any size, in teams of about five

Advance preparation: make letter cards and category cards

Materials: paper and pencils

Time frame: short

Write the letters of the alphabet on slips of paper, and put them in a basket. Write several categories on slips of paper and put them in another basket. You need at least as many categories as you have teams. Think of categories of things that have or need names: boys, girls, pets, cars, boats, plants, cities, streets, sports teams, restaurants, planets (discovered or otherwise), and so on.

Each team draws a letter of the alphabet from one basket, and a category from the other basket. They have three minutes to generate as long a list as possible of names in the chosen category that start with the chosen letter. Fact or fiction is immaterial, as long as the made up names start with the appropriate letter and clearly fit the category. The team with the longest list wins, though a team that chose "cars" and the letter Q might dispute the fairness of the process.

Rutabaga

Checklist

Group Size: any size

Advance preparation: none

Materials: none

Time frame: short

The particular combination of letters in the word "rutabaga" make it an interesting starting point for this fast-paced word and memory game.

Ask everyone to sit in a circle. One person starts by saying a word beginning with R: rancid. The next person says a word beginning with U, maybe ultimate. The next person says tailor-made, the next animal, the next banana, the next awful, then gargantuan, and finally, artistic. The person after that says rinse, the next person says ulterior, and the whole thing starts over.

Move fast. Any one who can't think of a word, who hesitates for too long, or who says a word not beginning with the correct letter, is out of the game. Those out of the game may not coach or make suggestions to those still in. No one may speak out of turn. No word can be used more than once.

Any word will do as the basis for this game. Choose one that has significance for your group. Use the guest of honor's name. Use the bridal couple's honeymoon destination. Use a word that represents a goal or accomplishment. Use the current month or day of the week. Use a movie or book title, the name of a musical group, or a favorite product. Think of a comical word, a philosophical word, or a word only people in your group would understand or find funny. Continue playing until nearly everyone has been eliminated, or until the momentum decreases.

All-Purpose, All Occasion

Here is a little grab bag of various icebreakers and energizers for use in any group situation. They may be timeless, season-less, and without a particular theme, but they are hardly bland. Some are active and physical, others relatively sedate. Some will provide a chuckle, and all will provide a break. Use them to provide a change of pace or a transition, or simply as entertainment.

Hiding

Checklist

Group size: up to about thirty

Advance preparation: none

Materials: seven marbles, buttons, or other small objects

Time frame: short

All participants stand in a circle. One person has all of the marbles. He or she walks around the circle, giving a marble to each of seven people at random. After distributing all the marbles, the marble holder leaves the room or stands away from the circle with his or her eyes covered.

For one minute, the marbles may be passed from person to person around the circle, quietly, and as unobtrusively as possible. At the end of a minute, everyone stands still. Whether or not participants are in possession of a marble, they hold out both hands in closed fists in front of them.

The marble holder then returns to the circle, with the task of figuring out who is or isn't holding a marble. Those standing in the circle must do their best to hide the location of the marbles; they may employ any means of deception they can think of, but they may not speak and they may not change the position of their hands, except to open them when asked to do so by the marble holder.

The marble holder has seven chances to locate all the marbles. If he or she does not succeed, the still hidden marbles stay where they are, and someone else may try to locate them. If the marble holder does succeed, the game moves to another round, with a new marble holder. Play as many rounds as you like.

Four Kinds of Tag

Checklist

Group size: any size, the more the better

Advance preparation: none

Materials: scarves for tail tag, otherwise none

Time frame: short

Tag, in almost infinite varieties, is time-honored, pure fun. A few minutes of it go a long way towards energizing or loosening up a group of people. For any version you want to play, make sure you have a large open space, cleared of obstacles, with some designated boundaries. You can set a timer to end the game, or play until everyone is exhausted, which won't take long.

TAIL TAG:

All players wear a scarf or something similar tucked into their belts, jeans, skirts, or whatever they are wearing, at the back. The scarf should be firmly anchored, but free-flowing, like a tail. The object is to steal other people's tails while protecting one's own. Players may not touch their own tails. Anyone who loses a tail may continue to play by stealing a tail and attaching it in the appropriate place. At the end of the game, anyone in possession of more than one tail is a winner, while those with no tails are the losers.

MOB TAG:

Star Trek fans might call this assimilation-by-the-Borg tag. One person is "it." As soon as he or she tags someone, they link arms, and together try to tag someone else. When they do, that person also links arms with them, and so on, until everyone is part of the mob. Resistance is futile.

INJURY TAG:

This is a free-for-all, in which everyone tries to tag everyone else, but avoid being tagged. Each time a player is tagged, he or she is injured at the tag location, and must treat the injury by placing a hand over the spot. Someone tagged on the shoulder, for instance, must play with one hand on the shoulder that was tagged. A person tagged a second time must play with a hand on each of the two tag locations. A person tagged a third time is dead, and out of the game.

FREEZE TAG:

One person is "it." Those he or she tags are frozen, and must stand perfectly still, in whatever position they happened to be in when tagged. Frozen players may be set free by the touch of an unfrozen player, so "it" tries to tag and freeze as many people as possible as quickly as possible.

Dots

With their eyes closed, participants should make six dots on the paper with the black marker. They then open their eyes, collect the papers, and redistribute them among the members of their small group.

Participants must then draw an object, and the drawing must make use of all six dots. They may talk among themselves, and share ideas, but each drawing must be original. It may not be an abstract design, but must represent something identifiable, however imperfectly.

Post the drawings, and award prizes for the funniest, most creative, most original, least convincing, and any other categories you like.

Raft

Use chalk markings, lines of rope, or small orange cones to define a "river" about eight feet wide and long enough to allow two teams to cross it by raft at the same time. Divide into two equal teams, each with a team leader.

This is a relay race. Team leaders, in possession of their cardboard rafts, start on the opposite bank of the river from their teams. The object is to get all team members across to that bank before the other team does.

In order to ferry their team members across, team leaders must first get to the other shore. They do this by sitting or standing on the raft, and maneuvering it in such a way that it moves forward across the river. Once they are close enough to the shore, team members may help pull them in.

Then, one by one, team leaders ferry their team members across the river. They may do this in one of two ways. Both team leader and team member may sit or stand on the raft and coordinate their efforts to maneuver it forward. In this case, team members on both sides of the river may help by either pushing them off or pulling them in once they are close enough. Or, the team leader may wade in the river, pushing or pulling the raft with the team member aboard across. In this case, no one on either shore may help at all.

The team leader may use either or both of these methods during the course of the game, but may not change methods mid-stream. When re-crossing the river alone to get another team member, the team leaders may not push or pull the raft, but must be on it, maneuvering it forward as best they can, as at the beginning.

Teams may not actively interfere with each other's progress. Anyone who falls or steps into the river, including team leaders who are not engaged in pushing or pulling an occupied raft, must return to the shore they started from and start over. The team that ferries all its members across first wins.

Seekers

Checklist

Group size: up to about thirty, in two equal teams

Advance preparation: none

Materials: one large, squishy ball; string, tape, or orange cones to mark the field

Time frame: short to medium

Place the ball in the middle of a large, open space, which will be the playing field. Mark the edges of the field with string, tape, or small orange cones. The teams line up along the sidelines of the field, but not on it. Each team chooses a volunteer, who will agree to be blindfolded, and in that condition attempt to find the ball and bring it back to the team.

After the seekers are blindfolded, a neutral person, acting as referee, moves the ball from the center of the space to some location of his or her choosing on the playing field. Both teams must refrain from giving away anything about the ball's new location until the referee blows a whistle, says "go," or gives some other signal that play may begin.

At that point, the blindfolded seekers begin moving toward the ball, guided by verbal directions from their teammates. No restrictions of any kind apply to these directions. Teammates may say anything they like if they believe their seeker will be helped by it. They may feel compelled to shout out their instructions in their efforts be helpful, and they may do so loudly with no penalty. They may not, however, physically enter the playing field or reach into it, and doing so will result in starting the round over.

The first seeker to locate the ball, pick it up, and carry it back to his or her team wins. But until the ball is safely in the hands of teammates, it is still vulnerable to the efforts of the other seeker, who might, still guided by his or her teammates, steal it. Play as many rounds as you like, using a new seeker each time.

Rin-tin-tan

Checklist

Group size: up to about thirty

Advance preparation: none

Materials: none

Time frame: short

This is a game that starts slowly and picks up speed and confusion as it progresses, especially if it's played late in the day, far into the evening, or after a certain amount of party libations have been consumed.

Sit together in a circle. One person starts. He or she simply says "rin," while placing a hand across his or her forehead and pointing to someone else in the circle.

The person pointed at places a hand over his or her heart and points at a third person, saying, "tin."

This person leans forward from the waist, as though bowing, points to someone else in the circle, and says, "tan."

The "tanned" person then silently points at yet another person, who starts over with another "rin," accompanied by the hand to the forehead while pointing to the next person in the sequence.

Anyone can be pointed to at any time, even someone who just had a turn. Anyone who makes a mistake, either in word or gesture, or who hesitates too long before responding, is out of the game. They aren't out of the fun, however. They can become hecklers, whose job it is to distract and confuse those still in the circle, using any means they can come up with except physical interference.

Play to a pre-announced time limit, until nearly everyone is out of the game, or until the momentum dies down.

ABC

Checklist

Group size: any size

Advanced preparation: none

Materials: paper and pencils

Time frame: short

Gather in small groups of about five people, and give each group a sheet of paper and a pencil. Instruct them to write the letters of the alphabet down the left hand side of the paper. Set a time limit of ten to fifteen minutes.

The goal is to find at least one object among the group members for each letter of the alphabet. The objects must be on a group member's person or in his or her possession, perhaps in a purse or briefcase, not at home on the kitchen counter or upstairs in the hotel room.

The objects may, however, be hidden from view; a person might claim an article of underwear, for instance, without being required to demonstrate its presence.

Body parts may be claimed, if participants are not too squeamish about it, as may physical markings such as moles, warts, birthmarks, and tattoos.

Adjectives may not be used to supply a letter, except in the case of colors; a blue shirt supplies the letter B, if desired, or the letter S. Likewise, an amethyst ring supplies either an A or an R, not both.

When the time is up, award prizes to the group with the most objects listed, to the group with the most letters represented, to the group that filled in a Q or an X, and to the group with the most creative entries. The grand prize, however, goes to any group which managed to fill in every letter.

Department of Silly Games

The existence of a department of silly games in no way implies an absence of silliness in games and activities not included in it. Like beauty, silliness is in the eye of the beholder. While it's not for everyone, or for every occasion, there are times when it's exactly right. For those times, here are a few silly games likely to engage even the silly-challenged.

Machines

Checklist

Group Size: any size, in teams of five to seven

Advance preparation: none

Materials: none

Time frame: short

Assemble in a large open space, where each team will have plenty of room to move around. The object is to create a machine, or something resembling a machine, by means of repetitive movements and sounds coordinated with those of other team members. The machine need not have a purpose, or even the appearance of a purpose. But it should look like it *might* have a purpose, and, if it did, it would be functioning properly. Don't bother to think this through, and take no time for planning.

One person on the team starts by making some kind of repetitive motion, accompanied by an appropriate sound. He or she might, for example, move an elbow back and forth while saying, "chugga, chugga, chugga."

One by one, the other people position themselves in relation to the first person, and then to each other, making repetitive motions and sounds of their own, in a way that suggests a smoothly running machine.

The second person might stand facing the first person, who is moving an elbow back and forth, and begin moving his or her knees up and down alternately, and in rhythm with the elbow mover, while saying "whoopa, whoopa."

The third person might stand in front of these two and move his or her shoulders up and down, saying "click, click, click." The fourth might kneel next to them, move his or her head back and forth, and say "thwack, thwack, thwack." What the fifth person might do is anybody's guess.

Once all the teams have created a machine, ask them to stop what they are doing, and then show off their machine's capabilities for the other teams. No explanations are necessary, but if a team believes it's machine has unique features, it may describe them. Teams may name their machines if they want to, and a prize may be given for the most creative or the most interesting or the most bizarre.

Farmyard

Checklist

Group size: any size, the more the better

Advance preparation: none

Materials: tokens, poker chips, pennies, or other small, flat objects

Time frame: medium

Divide into five or six teams, any number on a team. Each team chooses a leader. Assign each team a farm animal name: cows, sheep, pigs, horses, chickens, dogs.

Have about five tokens, poker chips, or pennies per player, and scatter them all over the floor of a large open area. On the word "go," everyone takes off looking for them.

Only the team leaders may touch the tokens with their hands. A team member who finds a token must place his or her foot on it and make the sound of the team's assigned animal until the team leader comes to claim it, at which point the player runs off to find another one. Team members may step on only one token at a time. The team whose leader collects the most tokens is the winner.

Cacophony and chaos are the primary results of this game, along with a good deal of laughter. If, however, your group is known for its cut-throat style of play, warn them of the possibility of physical injury if any one gets too aggressive in pushing others out of the way and stomping on tokens to claim them.

Pockets

Checklist

Group size: any size, in teams of about five

Advanced preparation: none

Materials: a long sock with a tennis ball stuffed into the toe

Time frame: variable

Gather in a large open area, preferably outside. Choose one person to be the tosser. The rest of the group forms teams of about five members each. Each team joins hands in a circle to form the "pockets." The pockets then line up along a starting line.

Standing behind the line of pockets, the tosser tosses the tennis ball/sock as high into the air as possible. The teams runs around underneath, trying to get it to fall into their pocket.

A team that fails to continually grasp hands during play is disqualified for that toss. A team that succeeds in getting the tennis ball/sock to land in its pocket wins two points. If the tennis ball/sock hits a team member, the team gets one point, whether the tennis ball/sock subsequently lands inside or outside the pocket.

Play to a pre-announced point limit; for example, the game is over when one team has five points, or three, or twelve. You can keep the same tosser through all the points of the game, or change tossers after each toss.

Colors

Checklist

Group size: any size

Advance preparation: none

Materials: large dot stickers in four different colors

Time frame: short

Give everyone four colored dots, one of each color, which they will place at various locations on their bodies. The only restriction as to location is that the dots must be visible. Each participant then chooses a partner.

At the command "red dot to red dot," participants must touch their red dots together. If one person has a red dot on his or her left shoulder, and the other person has a red dot on his or her right hip, touching them together might require some creative movements.

While attempting to continue touching red dot to red dot, participants must then follow the next command, which might be blue dot to blue dot, and so on. As in the old game of Twister, maintaining contact with all four combinations will lead to unlikely bending and twisting, and probably to some indelicate positions.

After the first round, participants find a new partner, and go through the four combinations again. They may not change the location of their dots between partners. Continue changing partners as long as you like. If you are doing this with people who don't know each other very well, allow some time for brief introductions before calling out commands.

Predator

Checklist

Group size: up to about thirty

Advance preparation: none

Materials: chairs, one fewer than there are participants

Time frame: medium

Divide the group equally into bunnies, fawns, and chipmunks. Arrange the chairs in a circle. One person, the caller, stands in the middle of the circle. Everyone else sits on a chair.

The caller's goal is to find a chair and get out of the middle of the circle. To accomplish this, he or she may call out commands which require the other players to get up and move around.

If the caller says "Bunnies!" for example, all the bunnies have to stand up and find a new chair; the same is true for fawns and chipmunks.

If the caller says "Forest fire!" everyone must stand up, grasp hands with someone else, run to the other side of the circle, and find a new chair.

If the caller says "Predator!" everyone must seek protection by hiding behind a chair, and then trying to find a new chair.

During the chaos which ensues after any of these commands, the caller has a good chance of finding a chair, leaving another player without one. That player becomes the new caller. Keep the game moving fast, and play as many rounds as you like.

Indiana Jones

Checklist

Group size: up to about thirty

Advance preparation: none

Materials: none

Time frame: medium

All players must remove their shoes for this game. If possible, play on a soft surface, such as a thick carpet or a gym mat. Players sit on the floor in two lines facing each other, their legs are outstretched, their feet just touching, their hands flat on the ground.

One person is "it." That person stands at one end of the two lines. His or her goal is to reach the other end by stepping over the legs and feet of the other players. The catch is that all of those players will be moving their legs up and down, like scissors, in their best imitation of a diabolical trap on the set of an Indiana Jones movie.

Play until everyone who wants a turn has one. Anyone who makes it through the line wins the opportunity to try again. Anyone who doesn't make it is dead, and therefore out of the game.

Cat and Mouse

Checklist

Group size: at least twenty, must be an even number

Advance preparation: none

Materials: none

Time frame: short

Play in a large open area, outside if possible. Designate one person as the cat, and another person as the mouse. Everyone else chooses a partner, the partners link arms, and all participants spread out as much as possible in the space available.

The cat, naturally, chases the mouse. The mouse may escape from the cat by linking arms with one member of a pair. That pair is now a trio, but it cannot remain so. The unlucky member of the pair with whom the mouse did not link arms must let go of his or her partner, becoming the new mouse.

If the cat catches the mouse, the mouse becomes the new cat, and the former cat must flee, joining a pair as quickly as possible, and making one member of that pair the new mouse. Play up to a pre-announced time limit, or until everyone seems tired out.

Index

Available from Brighton Publications, Inc.

Meeting Room Games: Getting Things Done in Committees by Nan Booth

Installation Ceremonies for Every Group: 26 Memorable Ways to Install New Officers by Pat Hines

Christmas Party Celebrations: 71 New & Exciting Plans for Holiday Fun by Denise Distel Dytrych

Folding Table Napkins: A New Look at a Traditional Craft by Sharon Dlugosch

Table Setting Guide by Sharon Dlugosch

Tabletop Vignettes by Sharon Dlugosch

Reunions for Fun-Loving Families by Nancy Funke Bagley

Games for Party Fun by Sharon Dlugosch

Romantic At-Home Dinners: Sneaky Strategies for Couples with Kids by Nan Booth/Gary Fischler

Kid-Tastic Birthday Parties: The Complete Party Planner for Today's Kids by Jane Chase

Games for Baby Shower Fun by Sharon Dlugosch

Baby Shower Fun by Sharon Dlugosch

An Anniversary to Remember: Years One to Seventy-Five by Cynthia Lueck Sowden

Games for Wedding Shower Fun by Sharon Dlugosch, Florence Nelson

Wedding Plans: 50 Unique Themes for the Wedding of Your Dreams by Sharon Dlugosch

Wedding Hints & Reminders by Sharon Dlugosch

Wedding Occasions: 101 New Party Themes for Wedding Showers, Rehearsal Dinners, Engagement Parties, and More! by Cynthia Lueck Sowden

Dream Weddings Do Come True: How to Plan a Stress-free Wedding by Cynthia Kreuger

Don't Slurp Your Soup: A Basic Guide to Business Etiquette by Elizabeth Craig

Hit the Ground Running: Communicate Your Way to Business Success by Cynthia Kreuger

These books are available in selected stores and catalogs. If you're having trouble finding them in your area, send a self-addressed, stamped, business-size envelope or call to request ordering information:

Brighton Publications, Inc.
P.O. Box 120706
St. Paul, MN 55112-0706

1-800-536-BOOK   http://www.partybooks.com